SAṂGAMA OF RELIGIONS

PANIKKAR'S CHRISTOLOGICAL PRAYāṆA 1

CHERIYAN MENACHERRY

Contents

PREFACE

Convergence of Religions: Panikkar's Christological prayāṇa 1, is the Indian Edition of the book published in Europe.[1]

According to Mahatma Gandhi there is no reason to believe that any historical figure was the incarnation of God or God as a historical figure was born in human or any other form. The statement reflects the general trend of Hinduism concerning the historicity of a divine mediator. Therefore, Jesus Christ as the only Mediator is often considered as a stumbling block in Hindu Christian dialogue. At the same time, in Hinduism, there is a longing for saviours, *avatars* who will be saving the world whenever the world is in peril. Hinduism expects a final avatar, *Kalki* for the end times for the destruction of the world. *Kalki*, the ultimate *avatar*, will destroy the present world order to liberate the world and humankind from the cycle of birth, death and rebirth and to grant ultimate liberation.

Many attempts have been made to view Jesus Christ in the context of the world religions, particularly of Hinduism. But Panikkar's is unique.

Panikkar observes that Christ must not be limited to the Christian mythical context, a saviour in history. Hindus speak of a transhistorical mediator having ten thousand echoes. Consequently, it will be more appropriate to describe the Christ mystery as 'cosmotheandric mystery'. Panikkar's insight is very helpful not only to foster Hindu Christian dialogue but also to pioneer an eco-Christology. In developing such a Christology, one may draw greater inspiration from Hinduism which, like the ancient Egyptian, Mesopotamian and European religions, is more intimately connected with nature. Almost all the sacred scriptures of Hinduism, either directly or symbolically or iconographically, allude to different aspects of nature and the cosmos.

While stressing the transhistoricity of Christ, Panikkar notes that Christ is not 'only' the historical Jesus. Jesus is the symbol of the Unknown Christ of Hinduism.

The series *Panikkar's Christological prayāṇa* presents the insights of Raimundo Panikkar especially his contribution in understanding the mystery of Christ from the perspective of world religions, especially Hinduism. *Convergence of Religions: Panikkar's Christological prayāṇa 1* is the first of the series. The series is the result of revision of my book *Christ: The Mystery in History: A Critical Study on the Christology of Raymond Panikkar* (1996).[2] The present book deals more about the semantics of Panikkar to understand his Christological insights; comprehensive bibliography of Panikkar is also included all in view of the forthcoming books of the series.

9th August 2024, on the feast of St Theresa Benedicta of the Cross (Edith Stein).

Prof. Dr. Cheriyan Menacherry CMI,

Bisingen, Germany

[1] Menacherry, Cheriyan. *Confluence of Religions, Panikkar's Christological prayāṇa 1*, Chisinau, Moldova: Blessed Hope Publishing, 2022.

[2] MENACHERRY, CHERIYAN. *Christ: The Mystery in History: A Critical Study on the Christology of Raymond Panikkar.* Peter Lang Publ Inc. (June 1996).

Sanskrit Glossary

Advaita. Non-duality, a non-dualistic philosophical view of reality, not to be confounded with monism

advitīyam. Lit. 'not having a second'

aham. I, the absolute I

ākāśa. Air, sky, space, ether, vacuity (emptiness), atmosphere, thefifth of the primordial elements (*mahābhūtāni:* earth, water, fire,air, ether) which is the element of sound. It is all-penetratingand infinite, hence frequently identified with Brahman

asya. 'of this' (Gen.)

ānanda. Joy, bliss, beatitude

anubhava. Direct experience, knowledge derived from immediate spiritualinsight

ātman. the Self

avatāra. 'decent', incarnation of Vishnu in animal or human form

avidyā. Ignorance

bhagavān. 'The blessed One', the Lord

bhāsya. Commentary

byāṣyakāra. Commentator

brahman. The Absolute, the World-ground

cit. Consciousness

darśana. Vision, world-view, philosophical system

dharma. Universal cosmic law, order, religion

dharmakāya. Lit. 'body of dharma or truth'. One of the three aspects which together constitute the Mahāyāna Buddhist conception of Tripple Body (*Trikāya: dharmakāya, nirmānakāya* or body of transformation and *Sambhogakāya* or Body of Bliss). The *dharmakāya* refers to the Buddha as the absolute, formless, ineffable realitywhich underlies all phenomena.[1]

dushṭa. Wicked

dvaita. Duality, dualism as philosophical system

eka. One, frequently *tat ekam,* the One as the origin of everything,later identified with Brahman

ekatva. Oneness

guṇa. Quality, property, etc. In the *Sāṁkhya* system the three'qualities' or fundamental constituents of *prakṛti* (nature), viz., *sattva* (modality of luminosity and intelligence), *rajas* (modality of motor energy and mental activity), *tamas* (modality of staticinertia and psychic obscurity)[2]

idam. 'this', the World

iṣtadevatā. The deity proper to a person or a group for worship and meditation; the chosen or proper deity

Īśvara. The Lord, God

janmādi. Origin etc.

jīva. The individual soul

jñāna. Knowledge, higher wisdom

ka. Interrogative pronoun 'who' one of the names of *prajāpati*

kali. The last and most degenerate of the four cosmic periods (*yuga*). We are now living in the *kaliyuga.*

Kālī. A goddess (other names: Satī, Pārvatī, Durga, Umā, Bhavāni), the *śakti* of Śiva. She also symbolizes eternal time and hence she both gives and destroys it.[3]

kalki. The tenth *avatāra* of Vishnu at the end of the *kali* *Yuga* ('dark age'). He will destroy a world sunk in corruption. After this destruction, Vishnu will rebuild the world anew.[4]

karma. Act, action, accumulated result of past actions

Kṛṣna. *Avatāra* of *viṣṇu* (lit. 'the black one') and one of the most popular of the Gods. He does not occur in the Veda, but it is he who reveals the BG

mahātmā. 'Great soul'; title of a sage or a saint

mahāvākya. The (traditionally four) Great Utterances of the Upaniṣads concerning *ātman* and *brahman.* Plural: *mahāvākyāni* simplified to *mahāvākyās*

mantra. Prayer, sacred formula, holy word, a Vedic text or verse

māyā. Divine power, power of illusion, World-illusion

mīmāṁsa. One of the six classical systems dealing mainly with thefoundations of and the rules for interpreting Vedic texts. *Pūrvamīmāmsa* deals with the ritual interpretation of the Veda. *Uttaramīmāmsa* or *Vedānta* gives a philosophical or spiritualinterpretation.

mokṣa. Liberation, salvation

nāma-rūpa. Name and form, the constituents of the reality World

Nārāyaṇa. The 'son of Man' (*nara*) i.e., of the original *puruṣa;* a namefor God in the form of Viṣṇu or Kṛṣṇa.

neti neti. 'not so, not so' referring to the ultimate reality or theSelf which can be expressed only negatively

nirguṇa. (Brahman) without attributes

nirvāṇa. Extinction, liberation (mainly in Buddhism)

om. The sacred syllable, consisting of the three letters A-U-M. It means also 'yes', 'so be it'.

prakṛti. Nature, primary matter; in Sāṁkhya one of the two fundamentalprinciples of the universe (*puruṣa* and *prakṛti*)

pāramārthika. The ultimate level, the ultimately real

paramātman. The supreme *ātman,* God; the term used to distinguish theuniversal from the individual *ātman*

prajāpati. 'The Lord of creatures,' the primordial God, Father of theGods and of all beings. His position is central in the Brāhmaṇa.

pramāṇa. Means of valid knowledge

prayāṇa. Journey, progress

puruṣa. Original, archetypal Man, Person

Rāma. *Avatāra* of Viṣṇu and one of the most popular Hindu Gods, themodel of righteousness.

ṛṣi. Sage, seer (of the Veda)

śabda. Sound, word. One aspect of Brahman as the revealed, manifestedone, *śabda-brahman*

saccidānanda. Brahman as Being (*sat*), Consciousness (*cit*) and Bliss(*ānanda*)

saguṇa. (Brahman) endowed with qualities. In Vedānta *saguṇa brahman* is equivalent of *īśvara*, the Lord.

śakti. Divine power, creative energy of the God, conceived in female form

sa,mhāra. Dissolution, destruction (of the World at the end of a cosmic period)

saṃsāra. Worldly existence, transmigration

saṃskāra. 'Sacrament', rites sanctifying the different stages of human life

sanātana dharma. 'Eternal religion', self-designation of Hinduism

sat. Being

Śvetaketu. Son of Gautama, a famous disciple of Uddālaka in CU to whom the highest teaching (*tattavamasi*) is imparted.

Śiva. The Auspicious One; in the Veda it is Rudra who, since the *Śvetāśvatara Upanishad* is known as Śiva, one of the most important Gods of the Hindu tradition

sṛṣṭi. Creation, emanation

śruti. 'That which has been heard', revelation of the Vedas, authoritative Scriptures of Hinduism *śūnyatā.* Void, absolute emptiness as the ultimate reality in Buddhism

sūtra. Lit. 'thread', short aphorism

tad. Demonstrative pronoun: that. Contrary to *idam* (this), it refers to Brahman. When occuring alone, it points to the ultimate reality without naming it. *tat ekam:* the One, that One

upamāna. Comparison, one of the 'means of knowledge' (*pramāṇa*)

vāc. The Word, speech, a sacred principle in the Veda

Vaiṣṇava. The cult of Viṣṇu, and a term for a follower of the cult. Vaiṣṇava is one of the three great divisions of modern Hinduism, the other two being the Śaiva and Śākta._[5]

veda. Lit. knowledge; the sacred knowledge incorporated in the Veda as the whole body of 'Sacred Scriptures'. In the narrow sense 'Veda' refers only to the Samhitās (*Rigveda, Yajurveda, Samaveda, Atharvaveda*); in the broader sense *brāhmaṇas, Aranyakas* and *Upanishads* are included. In the plural it refers to the four Vedas.

vedānta. Lit. 'end of the Veda,' i.e., the *Upanishads* as the culmination of Vedic wisdom. In the sense of *Uttaramīmāmsā* or *Vedāntavāda,* one system of Indian philosophy (*advaita Vedānta,* dvaita *Vedānta* etc.) based on the *Upanishads* and teaching a spiritual interpretation of the Vedas

viśiṣṭādvaita. Doctrine of 'qualified non-dualism', represented by Rāmānuja

Viṣṇu. The important God in Hinduism, already occurring in the Veda; his name means something like 'the all penetrating.' He is related to the sun. Later he becomes the second of the *trimūrti*, the preserver, and he is mainly worshipped in his *avatāras*.

vyāvahārika. Worldly reality, relative level

[1] E.J. Coleman, in *Abingdon Dictionary of Living Religions*, Gen. Ed., Keith Crim, (Tennessee: Abingdon, 1981), pp. 222, 768-769.

[2] Margaret and James Stutley, , *A Dictionary of Hinduism: Its Mythology, Folklore and Development* 1500 B.C.-A.D. 1500 (Bombay: Allied Publishers, 1977), pp. 243-244.

[3] Stutley, *A Dictionary of Hinduism:...* (1977), pp. 137-138.

[4] Vassilis G. Vitsaxis, *Hindu Epics, Myths and Legends in Popular Illustrations*, (Oxford: Oxford University Press, 1977), p. 63.

[5]Stutley, , *A Dictionary of Hinduism:...* (1977), p. 317.

I

The longing for the Saviour

In the beginning, according to Rigveda, *Prajāpathi* (lord of creatures) was born as a golden seed (*Hiraṇyagarbha*). He then became the Creator, the Lord (*Īśvara*) and the Saviour of the whole cosmos (X.121.1).[1] He pervades the whole cosmos by putting it on (X.121.10).[2] A part of Prajapathi, therefore, is mortal and another part is immortal (*amṛtam*) (X.90.2&8).[3]

Hinduism does not conceive of a Lord or Saviour incarnated exclusively in the form of a human being. Mahatma Gandhi stated: "There is no reason to believe that any historical figure was the incarnation of God or God as a historical figure was born in human or any other form."[4] The statement reflects the general trend of Hinduism concerning the historicity of a divine mediator. Therefore, Jesus Christ as the only Mediator is often considered as a stumbling block in Hindu Christian dialogue. At the same time in Hinduism there is a longing for saviours:

avatars who will be saving the world whenever the world is in peril. "Vishnu has ten avatars, of which his appearance as Rama and Krishna are arguably the most important. Vishnu's ten avatars are: as a fish, a tortoise, a boar, a man-lion, a dwarf, Rama with his axe (*Parasurama*), Rama with his bow (*Ramacandra*), Krishna, Buddha, and Kalki."[5] The expected final *avatar, Kalki* for the end times is for the destruction of the world.[6]*Kalki* the ultimate *avathar* will destroy the present world order to liberate the world and humankind from the cycle of birth, death and rebirth and to grant ultimate liberation.

Waiting for a saviour is not like waiting for the Godot as presented by Samuel Beckett. The human person has the desire for the saviour to come definitively. "Are you he who is to come, or shall we look for another?" (Mt 11:3; Lk 7:19-20) is the question that arises in one who expects God's direct intervention in the world. The saviour may not appear exactly the way a person expects. Naturally, John the Baptist wanted clarification from Jesus of Nazareth. The arrival of the saviour has a double effect: it corrects and fulfils the expectations of the people. Jesus Christ did this with Judaism, which expected a Messiah, but not one who suffers and dies: "A Messiah who suffers and dies as a substitute for all men in the NT sense was unknown in Judaism. To be sure, there is evidence for suffering *or* for death of the Messiah, but not for a Messiah who suffers *and* dies."[7] Jesus of Nazareth corrected and fulfilled the Judaic expectation of the Messiah: "the Son of Man must suffer many things, and be rejected by the elders and the chief priests and the scribes, and be killed..." (Mk 8:31). Peter wanted to remain in the Jewish idea of a Messiah who will not be suffering and dying and therefore rejected the foretelling by Jesus (Mk 8:32) about His suffering and death.

Jesus' rebuke to Peter in the presence of other disciples was also a correction to the Judaic notion about the Messiah and showed that suffering and death of the Messiah was God's plan (Mk 8:33). The people of Ancient Greece were open to the coming of an unknown god. But a god who dies and rises again was not to the taste of the people at the Areopagus. As Paul started to preach about the 'unknown god', the men of Athens were eager to hear him. But as Paul began to speak about "the resurrection of the dead some mocked" him. (Acts 17:22-34). It is very difficult for Hinduism to accept that Jesus of Nazareth fulfils the idea of the saviour. Does Jesus Christ also correct and fulfil the Hindu idea of the saviour?

Many attempts have been made to view Jesus Christ in the context of the world religions, particularly of Hinduism.[8] But Panikkar's is unique: "Perhaps no recent theologian in India or abroad has grappled with the question of Christ's relationship with the great non-Christian religions of the world such as Hinduism more than Raymond Panikkar."[9]

Panikkar observes that Christ must not be limited to the Christian understanding of a saviour in history. Hindus speak of a transhistorical mediator having ten thousand echoes. Consequently, it will be more appropriate to describe the Christ mystery as 'cosmotheandric mystery'.[10] Panikkar's insight is very helpful not only to foster Hindu-Christian dialogue but also to pioneer an eco-Christology. In developing such a Christology, one may draw greater inspiration from Hinduism which, like the ancient Egyptian, Mesopotamian and European religions, is more intimately connected with nature. Almost all the sacred scriptures of Hinduism either directly or symbolically or iconographically allude to different aspects of nature and the cosmos.

While stressing the transhistoricity of Christ, Panikkar notes that Christ is not 'only' the historical Jesus. Jesus is the symbol of the Unknown Christ of Hinduism. It is doubtful whether this approach does justice to the full Christian view of the Christ mystery which has to be presented in Hindu Christian dialogue, where authenticity to one's own faith is called upon from the dialogue partners. In fact, it is the experience of the Mystery in history which is central to Christianity. This centrality of Christian faith has necessarily to be shared when dialoguing with other religions. Jesus Christ shows that to share history is not to shed mystery. Christ is mystery in history.

Hinduism stresses the mystery of the mediator *Īśvara*,

Christianity adds the historicity of Christ. However, a closer look at Hinduism reveals the fact that a sense of history and the expectation of a saviour in history are not totally alien (even if not central) to the Hindu religion. Similarly, dialogue will bring to light more insights about the mystery dimension of Jesus Christ as, for instance, the enigmatic problem of the hypostatic union. This union, however, can more easily be understood by the Hindu mind if it is explained in terms the _advaitic_ union.

[1]"In the beginning there arose the Golden Child (_Hiraṇyagarbha_); as soon as born, he alone was the lord of all that is. He established the earth and this heaven:--Who is the God to whom we shall offer sacrifice?" (*Rigveda* X.121.1.)

[2]"O Prajapathi! you alone pervade all these created things, and none besides you." (*Rigveda*, X.121.10.) See also the comment by O.M.C.Narayan Namboothiripad, <u>Rigvedam: Bhashabahshyam</u> Vol. VIII, (Trichur: Kairali Press), 1986, p. 781.

[3]"all creatures are one-fourth of him, three-fourths immortality (*amṛtam*)" (X. 90, 2 and 8). In Śatapatha Brāmana it is said "...of that Prajapathi one-half was mortal, the other immortal...."(X.1.4.1). As given by A.C.Clayton, *The Rigveda and Vedic Religion*, Varanasi: Bharathi Prakashan, 1980, p. 90.

[4]Gandhi, *The Collected Works of Mahatma Gandhi*, New Delhi: Publications Division, Government of India, Vol. XXXVI, p. 165.

[5] Wilson, Tom. *Christian Responses to Five Views of the Bhagavad Gita*: Entry into Dialogue, Newcastle upon Tyne: Cambridge Scholars Publishing, 2021, p. 6.

[6] Cf. Wilson, *Christian ...Views of the Bhagavad Gita*, 2021, p. 6.

[7]E. Jenni, „Messiah, Jewish," in *The Interpreter's Dictionary of the Bible*, Vol.3 edited by George Arthur Buttrick, Nashville (USA): Abingdon Press, 1982, p. 365, cl. 1.

[8]Some of the literature in this field: J. Daniélou, sj. *The Lord of History: Reflections on the Inner Meaning of History* (London: Longman, Green and Co Ltd, 1958), pp.116-121, 124-129, 333-340. K. Rahner, „Christianity and the Non-Christian Religions" in *Theological Investigations. Vol.5: Later Writings*, trans. by Karl-H. Kruger (London: Darton, Longman & Todd Ltd. (1966) 1984), pp. 115-134. K. Rahner, „Jesus Christ in the Non-Christian Religions," in *Theological Investigations. Vol. XVII: Jesus, Man, And The Church*, trans., by Margaret Kohl (London: Darton, Longman & Todd, 1981) pp. 39-50. V.Chakkarai, *Jesus the Avatar* (Madras: CLS, 1932). Robin Boyd, *An Introduction to Indian Christian Theology* (Madras: The Christian Literature Society, 1979), p.6. J. Dupuis, sj._*Jesus Christ and His Spirit* (Bangalore: Theological Publications in India, 1977) pp. 179. Aloysius Pieris, „Speaking of the Son of God in Non-Christian

Cultures, e.g., in Asia", in *Concilium: Religion in the Eighties,* edt. by E. Schillebeeckx and Johannes-Baptist Metz (Edinburgh: T.& T. Clark Ltd. 1982) pp. 65-69. H. Küng. „The World Religions in God's Plan of Salvation." in *Christian Revelation and World Religions,* ed. J. Neuner. London: Burns and Oates, 1967, pp. 67-122. H. Küng; J. Van Ess; H. Von Stietencron; and H. Bechert, *Christentum und Welt-Religionen. Hinführung zum Dialog mit Islam, Hinduismus und Buddhismus,* (München Zürich: Piper, 1984), pp. 373-408. Bede Griffiths, *The Marriage of East and West* (London: Collins Fount Paperbacks, (1982) 1983), pp.172-192. Bede Griffiths, *Return to The Centre* (London: Collins Fount Paperbacks, (1976) 1984), pp. 83-146. Bede Griffiths, *The Cosmic Revelation* (Bangalore: Asian Trading Corporation, (1983) 1985). Bede Griffiths, *Christ in India: Essays Towards a Hindu Christian Dialogue* (Bangalore: Asian Trading Corporation, 1986).

[9]A. Karokaran, *Evangelization and diakonia: A Study in the Indian Perspective* (Bangalore: Dharmaram Publications, 1978) pp. 140.

[10]One of the inspirations for describing Christ as the cosmotheandric mystery is of course *Rigveda,* X.121.10. Cf. Panikkar, *The Vedic Experience: Mantramañarī,* (London: Darton, Longman & Todd, 1979, p. 70.

II

Raimundo Panikkar

Born in Barcelona on 03 November 1918, as the son of a Spanish Roman Catholic mother and an Indian Hindu father, Raimundo Panikkar had from the first an openness to these two religions.[1] He was ordained in 1946.[2] After his ordination "he left Spain in 1953 and lived in India until 1960, where he taught Indological subjects in the universities of Mysore and Banaras."[3] His work as a Roman Catholic priest in the diocese of Varanasi, enabled him to come into closer contact with the people of India, with their culture and their religions, particularly with the religion of his father.

He holds three doctorates: in science, philosophy and theology. In science, he specialized in chemistry, completed his Ph.D. at the University of Madrid in 1958.[4] After his brief engagements in scientific and industrial fields, he involved in psychology, philosophy and religion. And after the war, he took an active part in the cultural life of Europe in Spain.[5] During 1943-45 he was Assistant to the Chair of Psychology, Madrid. His doctorate in philosophy was from the University of Madrid in 1946.[6] During 1946-51, he was Professor for Indian Culture and Comparative Cultures in Madrid. In 1950-51 at Madrid and in 1962-63 at Rome, he was Professor of Religious Sociology. In 1952-53 he was Professor of Philosophy of History, Madrid; during 1967-71, he was visiting Professor of Comparative Religion at Harvard; In 1963, he was *Libero Docente* for Philosophy of Religion at Rome; In 1971, he was Professor of Comparative Philosophy of Religion and History of Religions at California. He has also taken part in various international lecture series: for example, he was the Delegate of UNESCO's Colloquium on Oriental Studies at Buenos Aires. With a dissertation on the relation of Christianity and Hinduism he got doctorate in theology in 1961 from the Pontifical Lateran University, Rome.[7]

He collaborated with different Journals especially on culture and religion.[8] The bulk of Panikkar's writings, with over 60 books and over three hundred major academic articles, and also innumerable public talks[9] were mainly concerned with comparative cultures, the history of religions, comparative religion, theology and hermeneutics.

After his retirement in 1987 and taking up residence in Tavertet, he founded Vivarium, centre of Intercultural Studies, today known as 'the Vivarium Raimon Panikkar Foundation'. In 2004, Panikkar took part in the Parliament of World Religions. The same year 2009 in which Barcelona awarded Panikkar the God Medal of Cultural Merit, he publicly presented his complete writings at the CaixaForum in Barcelona.

Raimundo Panikkar died at Tavertet in 2010.[10] Panikkar had a Christian and a Hindu funeral rite. The

Christian funeral rite was presided over by the bishop of Vic, and was held in the church of Tavertet on 28 August. According to his wish, his body was cremated. On the 04 December, a part of his ashes was buried in the graveyard near the parish church of Tavertet. And on 08 January 2011, the other part of his ashes was brought to Varanasi. Subsequently, the ancient Indian funeral rite of the "immersion of the bones" (*asthivilaya*) took place, conducted by a pundit. While spreading the ashes, contained in a vase, in the sacred waters of the Ganges, the last verses of Isha Upanishad were recited by the *pandit* in Sanskrit, the same verses, which decades ago in this place, Raimundo had translated."[11]

As one who has grown up and worked both in the East and in the West, he has had the rare opportunity of internalizing the essence of both Christian and Hindu traditions.[12] His involvement in other religions is so deep that he could rightly say that he started as a Christian, went through Hinduism and returned to Christianity, but only after passing through Buddhism. "Thus I am at the confluence (*sangam*) of the four rivers: the Hindu, the Christian, the Buddhist and the Secular traditions."[13]

[1]For the biographical information I am depending mainly on Panikkar, Curriculum Vitae: List of Books and Selected Articles (Santa Barbara [manuscript], 1984), pp. 2-6; also Cf. E.H. Cousins, „Introduction: The Panikkar Symposium at Santa Barbara." *Cross Currents* 29 (Summer 1979), pp. 132.

[2] Cf. E. H. Cousins, „Introduction:...," *Cross Currents*, 29 (Summer 1979) p. 132.

[3] Panikkar, „Letter to an Indian Christian Artist", 1956 Liturgical Art 32 (November 1963) p. 9 (in the Editor's note.

[4] E. H. Cousins, „Introduction:...," *Cross Currents*, 29 (Summer 1979) p. 132.

[5] „After a scientific and industrial experience he became professor of philosophy and took an active part in cultural life of Europe immediately after the war, mainly in Spain." Panikkar, „Letter to an Indian....," [1956] *Liturgical Art* 32 (November 1963) p. 9.

[6] E. H. Cousins, „Introduction:...," *Cross Currents*, 29 (Summer 1979) p. 132.

[7] E. H. Cousins, „Introduction:...," *Cross Currents*, 29 (Summer 1979) p. 132.

[8] Moreover, he was and is associated with different Journals on Culture and Religions, for example: he was the Vice-Director and one of the three founders of *Arbor*, a general Journal of Culture, Science and Philosophy, Madrid. Cf. Panikkar, Curriculum Vitae:..., (1984), pp. 5-6.

[9] Cf. Ignasi Moreta, „Raimon Panikkar: an intense life, intercultural thought," in Barcelona Metropolis,

https://www.barcelona.cat/bcnmetropolis/2007-2017/en/

[10] Cf. Ignasi Moreta, „Raimon Panikkar: ...," in Barcelona Metropolis.

[11] Maciej Bielawski, „Panikkar: His Life and His Works," Campo Dei Fiori, 2018.

[12]Cf. C. Bhattacharya, review of *The Intra-Religious Dialogue*, by R. Panikkar, in *Religious Education*, 74, Nov-Dec. 1979, p. 679.

[13]Panikkar, *The Unknown Christ of Hinduism: Towards an Ecumenical Christophany*, London: Darton, Longman & Todd; and New York: Orbis Books, 1981, p. x.

III

Scattered building blocks

The present and future generations are thankful to Panikkar for inheriting his vast ingenious contribution from the perspective different religions especially Hinduism.

A. Synthetic method is needed

Panikkar has produced "fundamental building blocks"[1] for a new theology, particularly a new Christology in the ambience of the world religions. Though the building blocks are lying scattered one can find important materials for the development of the two important and distinctly Christian doctrines: the Trinity and Christology. According to Coward, reality has, as its basic structure, two poles: "the God or transcendent pole, and the world." Trinity expresses God pole, upon which hinges the "God's action towards the world: in the origin of creation, revelation, Christology, redemption, grace, the church, and eschatology."[2] In Christology again reflects the two poles: God and world. Christ the Son of God as the Son of Man is in space and time. Through the Word the world was created. God sent His only Son in to the world to save it, to lead it from and through history to trans-history. The fallen humanity is the essential part of the redemption enacted by the Christ-event: its "restoration, sanctification, and salvation".[3] The building blocks that Panikkar has produced towards a "doctrine of Trinity which relates to world religions" is far advanced compared to his Christological thinking. Thus, he has "has provided, at least implicitly, all the building blocks of complete systematic theology. In addition, he has developed explicitly a number of the elements in the world pole of the structure, for example, the doctrine of man and of history."[4]

As Panikkar has not assembled the building blocks "together and shaped them into the classical genre of systematic theology,"[5] he has bequeathed the present and future theologians to bring the blocks together to form a synthesis as necessary in order to understand his ideas for a Christology in the Hindu religious context. For such a task E. Cousins calls to search through the writings of Panikkar to find out the building blocks suitable for making a new theology.[6] Thus the Christian theological community can continue the task pioneered[7] by Panikkar using his theological insights.

A. **Christological contributions**

The present book *Confluence of Religions* and the forthcoming books of the series *Panikkar's Christological prayāṇa* are mainly to understand insights of Panikkar on

Christology, as he tries to understand the Christ mystery in the context of world religions, particularly that of Hinduism, using the categories of history, symbol and myth. The scope here is not to examine the statements of Panikkar concerning Hindu religion or Philosophy: for instance, whether the *advaitic* Hinduism is the major, if not the sole, face of present-day Hinduism; or how Hinduism itself would evaluate the interpretation that Panikkar gives to their religious concepts, such as his attribution of different meanings to *Īśvara* by the new interpretation of Brahma-Sūtra I,1,2.[8]

i. **Panikkar's Semantics:**

When studying Panikkar, there arises the problem of his use of language.[9] For example, when he says myth, history, symbol etc., the meanings are different from an average understanding of them. "He is partial to terms like `analogical level' and `essential realm' and such neologisms as `ontonomy,' `iconolatry,' `ontic-intentional,' `dogmaolatry,' etc. He enjoys making up his own words..."[10] Panikkar's neologisms may puzzle the readers, and his use of the traditional words may confuse and give rise to semantic problems. Often, he stretches the usage of traditional words and charges them with new meanings. He does this also in his Christological terminology. There is the need for clarification and standardization of terms.

ii. **Words: 'Jesus', 'Christ'**

Panikkar uses Christ for the Son, for the Logos, for the Mediator, for the only mediating mystery, etc. The following is an instance: "`Jesus' is not the revealed name but he reveals the Supername".[11] "'Christ,' here, is not meant to refer specifically to Jesus of Nazareth but to the Logos, Principle, or Being that the various religious traditions call by a variety of names."[12] "Christ is not the revelation, not the revealed name but the revealer of the name."[13] "The whole Christ is Alpha and Omega, the beginning and the end, first begotten of the Absolute."[14] Christ is a reality transcending Christianity "for which Christians have no other name than Christ."[15] „Christ is an ambiguous term.... One may identify it with the Logos and thus the Son or equate it with Jesus. The nomenclature that I personally would like to suggest in this connection is as follows: I would propose using the word Lord for that Principle, Being, Logos or Christ that other religious traditions call by a variety of names and to which they attach a wide range of ideas.... Each time that I speak of Christ I am referring (unless it is explicitly stated otherwise) to the Lord of whom Christians can lay claim to no monopoly."[16] The name of Christ expresses „that ever hidden, though liberating, mystery which transcends all names."[17] „....the Son, Being and the Christ, he through whom and for whom everything was made,..."[18]

Therefore, according to Knitter, 'Christ', for Panikkar, „is synonymous with 'God the Son, the Logos',„[19] and also „both symbol and substance of this dynamic non-dualistic unity between God, humanity, and world. Christ, therefore, is synonymous with „God the Son, the Logos."[20] But sometimes Panikkar uses Christ, Jesus and Jesus Christ in the same sense: In that name [*Christ*] „all the treasures of the Godhead dwell in a most corporeal manner (Cf. Col., II, 9.)"[21] In another place he writes „....out of the people of Israel was born *Jesus* [italics mine] in whom the fullness of the Godhead dwelt in a corporeal manner (Cf. Lk. 3:22; Col.

2:9)."[22]

In the present book and the forthcoming books of the series *Panikkar's Christological prayāṇa*, therefore, the method of the use of the terms 'Jesus' and 'Christ' is the following: When dealing with Panikkar directly [except in direct quotation] the terms --Jesus, Christ and Jesus Christ-- stand mainly for a historical individual[23] having a special relation with the Divine Mediator, the Son. Christ is not a monopoly of Christians.[24] „Christ the Lord and Saviour is for the Christian the symbol of that mystery which is unveiled in or through Jesus."[25] That means Panikkar also uses Christ, not specifically to refer to Jesus of Nazareth,[26] but as the Mystery, the Supername,[27] the unique redeemer, the Logos, the Principle, the Being, the Lord, the Son, whom „the various religious traditions call by a variety of names".[28] In order to specify that, I capitalise the term whenever it occurs [except in direct quotation] in the present book and the forthcoming books of the series *Panikkar's Christological prayāṇa*: CHRIST.

[1]E. Cousins, „Raimundo Panikkar and the Christian systematic theology of the future." *Cross Currents* 29 (Summer 1979), p. 146.

[2] E. Cousins, „...Theology of the future," *Cross Currents*, 29 (Summer 1979), pp. 146 147.

[3] E. Cousins, „...Theology of the future," *Cross Currents*, 29 (Summer 1979), pp. 146 147.

[4] E. Cousins, „...Theology of the future," *Cross Currents*, 29 (Summer 1979), pp. 146 147.

[5]E. Cousins, „...Theology of the Future," *Cross Currents* 29 (Summer 1979), p. 146.

[6]„It is necessary, then, to search through his writings and to identify these building blocks. By analyzing them concretely, we will be able to discern the qualities of this

new theology....Having identified and analyzed these foundational elements, we can explore how they might be constructed into the classical genre of systematic theology, and we can observe how this genre will be transformed in the process." E. Cousins, „....Theology of the Future," *Cross Currents* 29 (Summer 1979), p. 146; cf. also p. 153.

[7]E. Cousins, „....Theology of the future," *Cross Currents*, 29 (Summer 1979), p. 154.

[8]Panikkar, *The Unknown*....., (1964), pp. 65-126. Panikkar, *The Unknown*..., (1981), pp. 97-162. See below II.F.2.c. The CHRIST, the Lord and *Īśvara*

[9]Panikkar, „Hermeneutics ...Religion:..," *The Journal of Religious Studies* VI, (Spring 1978), p. 45.

[10]W. Capps, „....the World's Religions," *Cross Currents* 29 (Summer 1979), p. 167.

[11] Panikkar, *Salvation in Christ:...*, (1972), p. 56.

[12] H. Coward, „Panikkar's...Dialogue," *Cross Currents*, (Summer 1979), p. 185. Cf. Panikkar, *The Trinity...*, [1970] (1973), pp. 53-54.

[13] Panikkar, *Salvation in Christ:*. (1972), pp. 61-62.

[14] Panikkar, „Dialogue between Ian and Ray: Is Jesus Christ unique?" Raimundo Panikkar and Ian Stephens, *Theoria to Theory*, I (Jan. 1967), p. 131.

[15]Panikkar, *The Unknown*....., (1981), p. 5.

[16] Panikkar, *The Trinity...*, [1970] (1973), p. 53.

[17] Panikkar, *Salvation in Christ:...*, (1972), p. 16.

[18] Panikkar, *The Trinity...*, [1970] (1973), p. 69.

[19] P.F.Knitter, „Theocentric Christology," *Theology Today* 40 July 1983, p. 135.

[20]P. Knitter, *No Other Name? A Critical Survey of Christian Attitudes toward the World Religions* (London: SCM Press Ltd 1985), p. 155

[21] Panikkar, *Salvation in Christ:....,* (1972), p. 62.

[22] Panikkar, *Salvation in Christ:....,* (1972), p. 65.

[23]„`Jesus' is not the revealed name but he reveals the Supername". Panikkar, *Salvation in Christ:....,* (1972), p. 56. „Christ is not the revelation, not the revealed name but the revealer of the name." Panikkar, *Salvation in Christ:....,* (1972), pp. 61-62.

[24] „The adjective `Christian' does not denote a monopoly of prerogatives reserved for the adepts of Christianity but...it indicates anything endowed with the richness of that reality for which Christians have no other name than Christ." Panikkar, *The Unknown.....,* (1981), p. 5.

[25]Panikkar, *Salvation in Christ:....,* (1972), p. 59.

[26]„`Christ,' here, is not meant to refer specifically to Jesus of Nazareth but to the Logos, Principle, or Being that the various religious traditions call by a variety of names." H. Coward, „Panikkar's...Dialogue," *Cross Currents,* (Summer 1979), p. 185. Cf. Panikkar, *The Trinity...,* [1970] (1973), pp. 53-54.

[27]Panikkar „invites the reader to a contemplative insight into that Mystery that can only be named in the vocative and whose name is a Supername chiselled upon a white pebble that can be properly kept only in the cave of heart--of the World." Panikkar, *The Unknown...,* (1981), p. xi.

[28]„`Christ,' here, is not meant to refer specifically to Jesus of Nazareth but to the Logos, Principle, or Being that the various religious traditions call by a variety of names." H. Coward, „Panikkar's...Dialogue," *Cross Currents,* (Summer 1979), p. 185. Cf. Panikkar, *The Trinity...,* [1970] (1973), pp. 53-54.

IV

Meeting of Religions

Unity, love and peace: this is humanity's ardent desire. Christian faith in one God--Father, Son and Holy Spirit-- is a faith not only in the love and union in the Trinity, but in this love and union as communicated to humanity (Jn 15:9, 17: 26). This unity, love and peace must be realized in all aspects of human society. It is indisputable that religious controversies are the major reasons for the disunity of humanity. Hans Küng stated that in order to avoid the wars of religions, which the globe is riddled with, we must be able to speak as brothers and sisters even about those points which seem to us indisputable and non-negotiable. According to him there will be „no world peace without peace among religions, and no peace among religions without dialogue between the religions, and no dialogue between the religions without accurate knowledge of one another".[1]

A. Unity in the heart of all religions

Raymond Panikkar made a clarion call for this union and synthesis of the religions of the world some decades ago, and saw this as „the *kairos* of our time".[2] He teaches that this unity must happen not at the end of time but in history itself. It is not enough to postulate this unity in the transcendental or eschatological realm. God is one, humankind is one. The unity of humankind is also historical. This means that humanity, in its pilgrimage, is somehow one. Humankind is realizing this unity in and through 'time'. No human person is an isolated particle. All are united as if in a magnetic field. Not only are all united to God but also the universe and human persons are united to each other. There is an „ontic Gemeinschaft der Lebewesen"[3] (ontic community of living beings). This urge towards unity is rooted in human nature. It is also in the heart of every religion. So also, the religions of humankind must converge in history. God is present in all religions. This God leads all men to salvation and brings together every fragment of this universe in Himself.[4] Unity means the existential and real oneness of God that exists in different religions and the plurality of the world.[5]

i. Plurality calling for Harmony

„Pluralism is a modern word standing for the old and perhaps abused term of *mysterion*. It is an emerging myth--and certainly it does not belong to the order of logos but of myth."[6] Ours is a pluralistic world. There is no escape from our geographical, climatic, cultural and political differences and divisions. The religions also are not exempt from it.[7]

As there is plurality in humankind, one has to admit that in the vast human cultures there are not only division and diversity but also an inspiring, inner, hidden unity. Anthropology accounts for this apparent plurality and hidden unity. It does not satisfy humankind with the existing plurality and diversity, its spirit always spontaneously strives to bring about harmony and unity.[8] Not remaining in their closed cells, people come out to meet their neighbours, to share their food and thinking.[9] Consciously or unconsciously, there is a tendency towards synthesis in humankind. Such a common human culture is not totally independent of the religions.

Culture is perhaps the external expression of religion. One can even say that culture is a secular religion.[10] If culture is one of the external aspects of religion, the striving for unity can also be traced back to religion. A fundamental aspect of all religions (without excluding either Buddhism or atheism) is the search for a fundamental union, a union between God and human person.[11] Ultimately, human beings have the same aspiration and the same fulfilment, because all have the same nature. This also leads one to think that the ultimate source with which people want to have communion, and to have fulfilment, is the same. That means the different ways to God ultimately join in one.[12] When a pure, white beam of light (God) falls on the prism of human nature, it takes different wavelengths, and multiple colours are produced.[13] The converse effect, the union of all colours into a white beam of light, is hoped for because they are, in fact, united at the source. If the religions are not already united, all our efforts at uniting them are in vain.[14] Panikkar may be hinting at the prayer of Jesus „...that they may be one even as we are one" (John 17: 22b) by using this image. This hints at the transcendental nature of the meeting of religions. Finding the basis for unity we are encouraged to work for this unity. It is more a mission than an achieved goal.[15]

i. Ecumenical Ecumenism for union, not uniformity

Panikkar believes that such union is not uniformity. But, at the same time, individuality must not be such as to threaten unity.[16] We must bear in mind the inner tension between unity and plurality. This tension between religions gives the possibility of unity by the ideal of ecumenical ecumenism. Panikkar visualised the ecumenical ecumenism as „the genuine and sincere encounter of religions following the example of Christian ecumenism. Christian ecumenism tries to reach a unity without harming diversity. It does not tally victors and defeated, but reaches a new point of agreement in deeper loyalty to a principle transcendent to the different Christian confessions. Ecumenical ecumenism attempts to reach a mutual fecundation and to allow a corrective criticism among the religious traditions of the world without diluting the unique contribution of each tradition."[17] Unity of religions will not be achieved by negating the inner tension.[18] Dankfried Reetz clarifies Panikkar's position: „In other words, the polarity between unity and plurality of religions is not overcome by abandoning one of the poles, namely plurality, but by undergoing the plurality and integrating it into the fulness of unity."[19] In fact, this polarity calls for a living historical dynamic, the existential growth of the religions to their whole fullness.[20]

iii. Unity as in the Mystery of the Trinity

For this inner tension of unity and plurality at the root of the encounter of religions in the very mystery of the Godhead, in the inner dynamism of the Godhead, the Trinity which „offers us the ultimate model" and the clue of this all-pervading constitution of reality, the unity and diversity.[21] „The Trinity as pure relation epitomizes the radical relativity of all that there is."[22] In the whole universe one can perceive the „radical inter-relationship of everything....These relationships encompass and constitute the entire web of reality." In the united human web of personal relations, there is a trinitarian structure: „the relationship expressed in the pronominal persons," I, Thou, and We.[23] One might well say that „it is in the trinitarian possibilities of the world religions" --„a fuller integration into human religious consciousness of the experience of the mystery and the life of the Trinity,"--[24] that Panikkar hopes for unity among religions. He urges Christians, without restricting themselves to a Mediterranean perspective,[25] to move forward in their approach to the universal unity of religions,[26] while keeping the tension between unity and plurality.[27]

Again, this meeting is more than an ideological agreement through, for example, a dialogue.[28] A real dialogue between religions will lead the partners into union as they both experience the same `currents' in the other's religion.[29] While commenting on Brahma Sūtra I.1.2 Panikkar says „It intends simply to open the door for a sincere dialogue by finding out the under-lying, or above-dwelling, reality... which both traditions are talking about."[30]

[1]H. Küng, „Christianity and World Religions: The Dialogue with Islam as One Model," (Paper read in the

Conference „Toward a Universal Theology of Religion" held at Temple University, Oct. 17-19, 1984, as quoted by Ann Marie Bahr, „Ecumenical Events: Toward a Universal Theology of Religion," *Journal of Ecumenical Studies*, 22 (Winter 1984), p. 197.

[2]Panikkar, *The Trinity and the Religious Experience of Man:Icon-Person-Mystery*, [1970] (London: Darton, Longman and Todd, 1973), p. 55. cf. pp. 5-6. Cf. Panikkar, *Kerygma und Indien. Zur heilsgeschichtlichen Problematik der christlichen begegnung mit Indien* (Hamburg: Herbert Reich, 1967), p. 9. Cf. Panikkar, *Kultmysterium in Hinduismus und Christentum: Ein Beitrag zur vergleichenden Religionstheologie* (Freiburg & München: Karl Alber, 1964), pp. 12-13.

[3] Panikkar, *Religionen und die Religion* [1964] (München: Max Hüber, 1965), p. 148

[4]Cf. Panikkar, *Religionen und die Religion* [1964] (München: Max Hüber, 1965), pp. 147-149.

[5]Panikkar, *Religionen....*, [1964] (1965), p. 150.

[6]Panikkar, *Salvation in Christ: Concreteness and Universality; The Supername*, (Santa Barbara, 1972), p. 2.

[7]Cf. Panikkar, *Kerygma und Indien.....*, (1967), p. 9. Cf. Panikkar, *Religionen.....*, [1964] (1965), p. 126.

[8]Cf. Panikkar, *Religionen.....*, [1964] (1965), p. 11.

[9]Cf. Panikkar, *Religionen.....*, [1964] (1965), p. 10.

[10]Panikkar, *Religionen.....*, [1964] (1965), p. 135.

[11]Panikkar, *Religionen....*, [1964] (1965), p. 12.

[12]Panikkar, *Religionen....*, [1964] (1965), p. 12.

[13]Panikkar, *Religionen....*, [1964] (1965), p. 151.

[14]Panikkar, *Religionen....*, [1964] (1965), p. 126.

[15]„Die Einheit der Religionen ist mehr eine Mission als eine Tatsache, mehr ein zu erstrebendes Ziel als ein Ziel, das schon erreicht ist." Panikkar, *Religionen....*, [1964] (1965), pp.

126-127.

[16] Panikakr invites us „to enter that path in which the divine depths and the human heights meet, where the necessary distinctions between philosophy and theology, matter and spirit, reason and faith, God and man, one religious tradition and another, are not blurred, but where they do not become lethal separations either." Panikkar, The Trinity..., [1970] (1973), p. xiv.

[17] Panikkar, „Have 'Religions' the Monopoly on Religion?" *Journal of Ecumenical Studies*, 11 (Summer 1974), p. 517. Cf. Panikkar, „Toward an ecumenical Ecumenism" *Journal of Ecumenical Studies*, XIX, 4 (Fall 1982), pp. 781-782.

[18]Cf. Panikkar, *Religionen....*, [1964] (1965), p. 11.

[19]D. Reetz, „Raymond Panikkar's Theology of Religions," *Religion and Society*, XV (September, 1968), p. 41.

[20]„...diese Polarität eine lebendige geschichtliche Dynamic her vorruft: das existentielle Wachstum der Religion zu ihrer ganzen Fülle." Panikkar, *Religionen....*, [1964] (1965), pp. 10-11.

[21]Panikkar, *The Trinity...*, [1970] (1973), p. xv.

[22]Panikkar, *The Trinity...*, [1970] (1973), p. xv.

[23]Cf. Panikkar, *The Trinity...*, [1970] (1973), pp. xv-xvi.

[24]Panikkar, *The Trinity...*, [1970] (1973), p. 55.

[25]„Diese heilsgeschichtliche chance stellt den Kairos des heutigen Christentums dar." Panikkar, *Kultmysterium....*, (1964), pp. 12-13.

[26]Cf. Panikkar, *The Trinity....*, [1970] (1973), pp. x-xi.

[27]Cf. Panikkar, *Religionen....*, [1964] (1965), p. 10.

[28]Panikkar, *The Unknown....*, (1981), p. 3. „I am only emphasizing that we meet in the center and not only in the periphery of social, legal, or even individual encounters--important as all these are." Panikkar,

„Response to Harold Coward," *Cross Currents*, (Summer 1979), p. 191.

[29]In fact it is not a real dialogue between religions. „Dialogue in the real sense arises precisely where I (or we) discover the same currents and problems within the religion of the 'other' as I (or we) find in my (or our) own religious world." Panikkar, „Advaita and Bhakti. A Hindu-Christian Dialogue," [1965] *Myth, Faith and Hermeneutics: Cross-Cultural Studies*, (New York: The Paulist Press, 1979), p. 278.

[30]Panikkar *The Unknown....*, (1964), p. 68.

V

The main background of Panikkar's study is formed of the broad scenario of world religions, especially the luxuriant world of Hinduism, and the general discussion on the philosophy and theology of religions.[1] For the cross-cultural understanding he found it necessary to explore the philosophical and religious traditions of India,[2] particularly of Hinduism. His thorough knowledge of Hinduism is displayed in one of his monumental works *The Vedic Experience*.[3] There, he masterfully explains the main trends of Hindu philosophy and its traditions. It is with this kind of deep religious experience and mastery of Hinduism that he enters into the interreligious dialogue.

A. Interreligious Dialogue

Humanity not only fought against but also is fighting for and in the name of religion. In this context „The dialogue among religions appears today more and more as a religious and human...imperative."[4] Panikkar finds the need for the interreligious dialogue not merely in the attempt to avoid conflicts between religions.

i) Mutual fecundation: the fifth *kairological* moment

The religions have now reached the fifth *kairological* moment, after passing through the other four kairological moments: „isolation", „indifference", „condemnation", „co-existence".[5] The fifth stage „mutual fecundation"[6] is for mutual transformation enriched by the other in the dialogue: „we enter into dialogue to be convinced, to be defeated and in this way to fecundate our partner and be transformed ourselves...."[7] The transformation can happen only if there are mutual correction and self-correction after encountering the other. In the stage of mutual fecundation, the religions can correct each other: „Dialogue does not mean primarily study, consultation, examination, preaching, proclamation, learning, etc., but if we insist on dialogue we should respect and follow its rules: it is not only there to listen and to observe; it is also there to speak, to correct and to be corrected; it aims at a mutual fecundation."[8] Together with correction there is mutual sharing of riches from the other religions.[9] This is because of the conviction that the other religious traditions are not to be totally refuted or not to be totally accepted. As a result, one is led to the „experience of discovering positive values in the other...." Breaking the idea of the invincible self-sufficiency of one's own religious tradition, one assimilates the complementary aspects in the other. „In short the 'other' becomes complementary to oneself."[10] The mutual enrichment is the „genuine Christian service is to fill out that `truth' of Hinduism without letting it lose its universality...."[11] It is also the genuinely Christian attitude „to call forth that 'truth' of Hinduism without destroying the latter's identity. To Christianity, Hinduism in turn offers the authentically Hindu gift of a new experience and interpretation a new dimension, in fact of the Mystery."[12] If Christian theology is formed mainly from the Hebraic, Greek and Roman cultural and philosophical background the other religions, for instance, Hinduism and Buddhism having a different cultural and philosophical background in developing their thoughts can contribute to Christianity to understand the ultimate mystery: „Perhaps the deep intuitions of hinduism and buddhism, which come from a different universe of discourse than the greek, may help us to penetrate further the trinitarian mystery. After all, is not theology precisely the endeavour of the man of faith to express his religious experience in the mental and cultural context in which he is situated?"[13]

Panikkar mainly „focused on the problem of the relationship between religions-- especially between Christianity and Hinduism."[14] Aware that „the correct approach to inter-religious dialogue is a matter of top priority for today's world,"[15] he began to conceive the basic principles for an effective dialogue between religions.[16]

ii) Dialogue: a revelatory and a 'conversion' experience

Quintessential for an effective interreligious dialogue are: respect and intellectual openness to the other religions,[17] an involved knowledge of the partner in dialogue. The partner of dialogue is a revelatory experience: „When you dialogue with somebody, look at your partner as a revelatory experience as you would-and should-look at the lilies of the field."[18] Dialogue call for a 'conversion' to others faith: „A Christian will never `understand` Hinduism if he is not con-verted to Hinduism. Never will a Hindu `understand' Christianity unless he becomes a Christian."[19] It is more or less this attitude that he expresses by the `Linguistic model' for dialogue. In order to translate one must enter into the language. One must be convinced of what one conveys. „The translator has to be also a speaker in that foreign language, in that alien tradition; he has to be a true spokesman for that religion;

he has to be, to a certain extent...convinced of the truth he conveys, converted to the tradition from which he translates. Here I am already in the intra religious dialogue."[20]

There must not be a bracketing one's own deep faith.[21] There should be loyalty and truthfulness to one's own religious identity,[22] by distinguishing between the peripherals and fundamentals of one's own faith. The „distinction between essence and form is vital nowadays as regards all religious awareness and notably as regards Christianity".[23] „The different issues--theological, practical, institutional etc.-have to be carefully distinguished."[24]

iii) Unity in the depth of religions

When all the religions enter deeply into their own identities, there is a chance of finding a deeper unity between religions. Panikkar puts forward analogies for this process: The rainbow model. The different traditions of humankind are like the almost infinite number of colours that appear once the simply white light of reality falls on the prism of human experience; it diffracts into innumerable traditions, doctrines and religions, through culture, geography and many other factors.[25] If in the rainbow model diffraction produces the religions, in the topological model transformation or deformation „is the cause of the different forms and shapes of geometrical figures, viz. of religions....In and through space and also due to the influence of time, a primordial and original form takes on an almost indefinite number of possible transformations through the twisting of Men, the stretching by history, the bending by natural forces and so on."[26] The different colours are ultimately derived from the one white light; and the geometrical or topological model, in which the hypothesis is that „all the various human ways come from a fundamental experience transformed according to laws, which have to be discovered. Or again, it might be that all religions are actually different until the topological transformations have been constructed."[27]

A.   Intrareligious Dialogue

A real interreligious dialogue is an intrareligious dialogue, a dialogue that proceeds „from the depths of my religious attitude to these same depths in my partner."[28] To have a thorough knowledge of the fundamentals of one's own religion is a precondition. Intrareligious dialogue is a precondition for interreligious dialogue: „No inter-religious dialogue can yield any fruit unless it is (at least logically and anthropologically) preceded by an intra-religious dialogue within the partners themselves."[29] That is: „The dialogue begins to take place within" oneself.[30] There should „an inner dialogue within myself, an encounter in the depth of my personal religiousness, having met another religious experience on...[a] very intimate level. In other words, if interreligious dialogue is to be real dialogue, an intrareligious dialogue must accompany."[31] The dialogue calls for constant renewal one's own religion: The intrareligious dialogue will satisfy the constant demands of the living Christian faith for „a total renewal, or in Christian terms a real, personal and ever recurring metanoia."[32]

In fact, to have to face up to the variety of world religions is a blessing. It enables one to go and examine the fundamentals of one's own faith: „Only others can help me to find out my presuppositions and underlying principles of my science. In one word, *das Ungedacte*, the unthought, can be disclosed only by him who does not `think' like me: he helps me to discover the unthought magma out of which my thinking crystallizes, and I on my part can do him the same service."[33] Dialogue context helps to have creative theologizing: „....all meaningful theologizing for the future must start from the fact of inter-religious dialogue as its necessary context."[34] Indeed, many of the developments of theology, particularly of the early Church, occurred in the context of the encounter of different religions.[35]

Panikkar followed in the footsteps of the early Church by situating himself in the world religious context. The function „of fundamental theology consists in providing a theological justification of a theological as well as a religious pluralism."[36] He tries to place the foundations of Christian theology „on a basis which at least makes sense for peoples living outside the cultural area out of which fundamental theology has traditionally grown."[37] „The role of fundamental theology is therefore to work out the intelligibility of theology also outside the culture and even the religion where that theology has until now grown and prospered."[38] But at the same time, he does not assume an apologetic attitude,[39] for he knows that we need not defend the Son of God; what we need is, with all humility, to enter deeply into the mystery of Christ working in other religions.[40]

Often the Christian interpretation of the religions of the world guided because „all that does not belong 'officially' and 'visibly' to historical Christianity, or to the Church, is sin and satanic (and extrapolation of the saying that everything not born of God is sin (Cf. Rom. 14:23)...."[41] Such an interpretation is contrary to the fact that „the Spirit of God has also been at work in other religious traditions (Rom. 10:10) and that even Christ, who is before Abraham

(Jn. 8:58), is somehow present and effective in those other religions. Lord, we have seen some performing miracles in your name who do not belong to our group....(Lk. 9:49; Mk. 9:38.). `The rock indeed was Christ!' (I Cor. 10:4)."[42]

Consequently, „no religion can boast to have deciphered fully the mystery of man and God."[43] Therefore, Panikkar tries to reinterpret, „to enlarge and deepen the mystery of the Trinity that it may embrace this same mystery existent in other religious traditions but differently expressed."[44]

By this special attitude he has been able to perceive and experience not only the greatness of his own Christian tradition, but also the worthy values in other religious traditions. No wonder he is in favour of the mutual fecundation of religions --seeking to enrich other religions while being enriched by them. At the mutual fecundation stage, he interprets „Christian doctrines in an interreligious context."[45] In this task he is not only taking „into account other religions but is profoundly enriched by them."[46] There is a reciprocity. Interreligious dialogue will, for instance, try to deepen the mystery of the Trinity and with deeper knowledge of the Trinity one can share mutually the Trinitarian experience of the other: „The deepening into the trinitarian structure of religious experience and of the human beliefs may here again offer a possibility of fecundation, agreement and collaboration not only among religions themselves, but also with modern man at large, so often torn apart by religious subtleties which he does not understand."[47]

[1]Panikkar, *The Unknown...*, (1964), p. xi.

[2]Cf. E.H. Cousins, „Introduction:...," *Cross Currents* 29 (Summer 1979), pp. 132.

[3] Pankkar, *The Vedic Experience. Mantraman~jarí: An Anthology of the Vedas for Modern Man and Contemporary*

Celebration [1977] (London: Darton, Longman and Todd, 1979).

[4]Panikkar, „Inter-Religious Dialogue: Some Priciples", *Journal of Ecumenical Studies* 12 (Summer 1975) p. 407.

[5]Panikkar, „Hermeneutics of Comparative Religion: Paradigms and Models." *The Journal of Religious Studies* VI, (Spring) 1978. pp. 39-40.

[6]Panikkar, „Hermeneutics...Religion:...," *The Journal of Religious Studies* VI, 1 (Spring 1978), p. 40. Panikkar, „Inter-Religious Dialogue:...," *Journal of Ecumenical Studies* 12 (Summer, 1975), p. 408.

[7] R. Panikkar, „Some words instead of response," *Cross Currents* 29 (Summer 1979), p. 194.

[8] Panikkar, „The Internal Dialogue--The Insufficiency of the so-called phenomenological 'Epoché' in the Relilgious Encounter," Religion and Society Vol. XV, No.3 (September 1968), p. 64."

[9]Panikkar, „Metatheology or Diacritical Theology as Fundamental Theology," *Concilium*, (June 1969), pp. 26-27. Cf. Panikkar, *The Trinity*..., [1970] (1973), p. 55. .

[10] Panikkar, „Hermeneutics...Religion:...," The Journal of Religious Studies VI, (Spring 1978), p. 40.

[11] Panikkar, The Unknown..., (1964), p. xi.

[12] Panikkar, The Unknown..., (1981), p. 4.

[13] Panikkar, The Trinity..., [1970] (1973), p. 46. Cf. Panikkar, The Unknown...., (1981), p. 7.

[14]H. Coward, „Panikkar's Approach to Interreligious Dialogue." *Cross Currents* 29 (Summer 1979), p. 183.

[15]H. Coward, „Panikkar's Approach to Interreligious Dialogue." *Cross Currents* 29 (Summer 1979), p. 183.

[16]The main works of Panikkar in the field of interreligious dialogue are: „The Rhetoric of interreligious dialogue," Jeevadhara 8 (Kottayam 1978) pp. 367-380.

Panikkar, *The Intrareligious Dialogue.* (New York: The Paulist Press, 1978). „The Hermeneutics of Hermeneutics. Reflections on the hermeneutics of Tradition in Hinduism in view of a dialogue with Christian thought." [1963] *Philosophy Today* 2 (Fall 1967), pp. 166-183. „Advaita and Bhakti, love and identity in a Hindu Christian Dialogue," [1965] *Journal of Ecumenical Studies* 7 (Spring 1970) pp. 299-309. Panikkar, „The Internal Dialogue:..," *Religion and Society* XV, 3. (1968), pp. 55-66. „Witness and Dialogue," [1972] In *Myth, Faith and Hermeneutics:..,* (1979), pp. 231-256. „Inter-Religious Dialogue:..," *Journal of Ecumenical Studies* 12 (Summer, 1975), pp. 407-409. „The Sermon on the Mount of Intrareligious Dialogue," (Editorial), *Journal of Ecumenical Studies* 22 (Fall 1985) p. 773. „Hermeneutics...Religion:..," *The Journal of Religious Studies* VI, 1 (Spring 1978), pp. 38-51.

[17]Panikkar, *The Unknown...,* (1964), p. 3.

[18] Panikkar, „The Sermon on the Mount...," *Journal of Ecumenical Studies* 22 (Fall 1985) p. 773.

[19] Panikkar, *The Unknown...,* (1964), p. 11.

[20] Panikkar, *The Intrareligious Dialogue,* (1978), p. xxvi. Cf. also Panikkar, „Hermeneutics...Religion:..," The Journal of Religious Studies VI, 1 (Spring) 1978. pp. 49 50.

[21]Panikkar, „The Internal Dialogue:..," *Religion and Society* Vol. XV, No.3 (September 1968) p, 64.

[22]Panikkar, *The Unknown...,* (1964), p. 3. Cf. R. Panikkar, „The Sermon on the Mount...," *Journal of Ecumenical Studies* 22 (Fall 1985), p. 773. Cf. Panikkar, *The Unknown...,* (1981), p. 7, cf. p. 35.

[23] Panikkar, The Trinity..., [1970] (1973), p. 3.

[24] Panikkar, „Inter-Religious Dialogue:..," Journal of Ecumenical Studies 12 (Summer, 1975), p. 408.

[25] Panikkar, „Hermeneutics...Religion:..," The Journal of Religious Studies VI, (Spring 1978), pp. 46-47. Cf. Panikkar, The Intrareligious Dialogue, (1978), pp. xix xx.

[26] Panikkar, The Intrareligious Dialogue, (1978), pp. xxi xxii. Cf. also Panikkar, „Hermeneutics ...Religion:..," The Journal of Religious Studies VI, (Spring 1978), p. 47.

[27]Panikkar, „Hermeneutics ...Religion:..," *The Journal of Religious Studies* VI, (Spring 1978), p. 48.

[28]Panikkar, *The Intrareligious Dialogue*, (1978), p. 50, cf. also pp. 40-44.

[29]Panikkar, „Inter-Religious Dialogue:..,", *Journal of Ecumenical Studies* 12 (Summer 1975), p. 408. Cf. also Panikkar, „The Internal Dialogue:..," *Religion and Society* Vol. XV, No.3 (September 1968), p. 66. „The intercultural dialogue has to begin as an intra-religious experience." Panikkar, Curriculum Vitae:..., (1984), p. 2.

[30]Panikkar, „Hermeneutics ...Religion:..," *The Journal of Religious Studies* VI, (Spring 1978), pp. 40.

[31] Panikkar, The Intrareligious Dialogue, (1978), p. 40.

[32] Panikkar, The Intrareligious Dialogue, (1978), p. 52.

[33] R. Panikkar, „Metatheology...," *Concilium*, (June 1969), pp. 26-27.

[34]H. Coward, „Panikkar's...Dialogue," *Cross Currents*, (Summer 1979), p. 184.

[35]Panikkar, *The Intrareligious Dialogue*, (1978), pp. 58-62.

[36]Panikkar, „Metatheology...," *Concilium*, (June 1969) p. 25.

[37]Panikkar, „Metatheology...," *Concilium*, (June 1969), p. 23. Cf. Panikkar, *The Trinity*..., [1970] (1973), p. xiv.

[38]Panikkar, „Metatheology...," *Concilium*, (June 1969), p. 25.

[39]Cf. Panikkar, *The Unknown*..., (1981), pp. 56, 98-99. Cf. Panikkar, „Metatheology...," *Concilium*, (June 1969), p. 21.

[40] Panikkar, *The Intrareligious Dialogue*, (1978), p. 63.

[41] Panikkar, The Intrareligious Dialogue, (1978), p. 63

[42] Panikkar, The Intrareligious Dialogue, (1978), p. 63.

[43] Panikkar, The Unknown..., (1964), p. 4.

[44] Panikkar, The Trinity..., [1970] (1973), p. 42. Panikkar, The Unknown..., (1981), p. 2. Cf. Panikkar, Salvation in Christ:..., (1972), p. 67.

[45]E. Cousins, „Introduction: The Panikkar Symbosium at Santa Barbara," *Cross Currents* 29 (Summer 1979), p. 132.

[46]E. Cousins, „...Panikkar Symposium...," *Cross Currents*, (Summer 1979), p. 133.

[47] Panikkar, The Trinity..., [1970] (1973), p. xiv. Cf. also Panikkar, „The Hermeneutics of Hermeneutics...," [1963] Philosophy Today 2 (Fall 1967), p. 179.

VI

Towards Metatheology, Theology of religions

Interreligious dialogue, intrareligious dialogue and mutual fecundation fuel each other. Living in the context of different religions is a constant challenge that „demands from us a total renewal or, in Christian terms, a real, personal and ever-recurring metanoia."[1] From this interaction Panikkar visualizes a new theology, the theology of religions, or rather metatheology. The aim is to create a „theology of religion valid for more than one religious tradition".[2] Even though there are serious theological problems to clarify and one cannot foretell whether the effort at creating such a theology will succeed, it cannot be said to be an *a priori* impossible enterprise.[3] In the hermeneutics of theology, with his cross cultural experience, Panikkar wants to include „the diverse religious experience of mankind." For Panikkar „has been acutely aware of the limits of Western thought. Although trained in contemporary European hermeneutics, he has constantly warned against applying uncritically Western principles of interpretation to the diverse religious experience of mankind."[4] Thus, he gives the hermeneutical principles for theologizing in the world religious context.

There are two basic aspects to his hermeneutics for the theology of the future: „The first indicates that his hermeneutics operates in a cross-cultural religious context; the second, that his hermeneutics is rooted deeper than logos."[5]

The fundamental theology must be dialogue which transcends the Logos „by being a 'dia logos', a 'going through the logos' as it were, in order to decide which logos we are going to use and if at all the ground of our search belongs to the logos or to the Spirit."[6]

A. Spiritual experience central to theologizing

Panikkar includes in the hermeneutics together with the speculative the experiential aspect also, a meeting of West and East: Panikkar's „Theology is simultaneously experiential and speculative. It is rooted in experience, tapping the wellsprings of Christian spirituality at a point that can make contact with the depths of Oriental spirituality. This wealth of spiritual experience is then reflected upon with his rare gift for metaphysical speculation that draws both from the mainstream of Western European philosophy and the philosophical traditions of the East."[7] He „combines the polarities of the East and the West, outer and inner consciousness, science and mysticism, mythic and rational thinking, pragmatic involvement in the world and spiritual detachment."[8]

Oriental religions and theologies are rooted in deep spiritual experience. So also, Panikkar's point of departure is from a deep spiritual experience rather than metaphysics. This is unlike Aquinas or process theologians who depend on the metaphysics of Aristotle or Whitehead. Here Panikkar is more like Bonaventure or early Franciscan theologians „who took their point of departure from the mainstream of Christian spirituality." His sophisticated philosophy is „always derivative of a deeper level of spiritual experience". This trend of Panikkar's may be a corrective to the too speculative, systematic, philosophical character of Western theology.[9]

B. Mysticism in theologizing

The stress on the experiential aspect in the theology leads to the mystical dimension of Theology. Panikkar chooses „the language appropriate to meditation, such as springs from the intelligence by a contemplative affinity."[10] About his book *The Unknown Christ of Hinduism* he wrote: „The thesis of this book is a mystical one."[11] Panikkar draws inspiration from mysticism in different religions. As mysticism is present in the depth of all religions, it will be a bridge-maker between religions. It perceives the unity and totality of reality. The mystical aspect is relevant in all times, and this factor contributes to the vitality of all religions.[12]

Panikkar „has urged scholars to penetrate to the depth of religious experience--in its diversity--before beginning to interpret; and he has cautioned against a superficial `translation' across cultural and experiential boundaries."[13]

A. **Hermeneutical principles of metatheology**

Following is an attempt to categorise some of the hermeneutical principles, the major trends and guidelines, of Panikkar's metatheology that he himself stated on various occasions. Even though presented with different names, some of his norms are practically the same.

i. **Avoid Centrifugalism**

There is in every human person a trend towards transcending one's existing system or situation. This tendency gives a tolerant attitude towards other views and approaches. It helps to overcome provincialism. But it has its negative side as well. It tends to negate completely existing ways of acting.[14] The theology of religions is not a flight from one's existing religion. Metatheology does not negate one's own traditional theological categories.

i. **Centripetalism is insufficient**

Centripetalism positively helps to study in depth one's own religion. Its method is chiefly introspective, seeking the immanent kernel of one's own religion in order to be a good Hindu, a good Christian, etc. Do not worry now about the union of religions or a theology of religion. What is needed is to be true to one's own religion and its theology. In the end (not in this historical period) we will meet somehow.[15] The basic attitude here is the *autonomic*--shy away from all the outward interference in one's own affairs. Starting from the urge for autonomy it ends in rebellious independence and disconnection.[16] The world, human being, is „*sui iuris*, i.e. self-determined and determinable, each being a law unto its self. This autonomy means that any injunction from outside, even if it is said to come from above, is regarded as an abusive imposition."[17] Centripetalism is not open to other world views and religions. The basic principle of human interrelatedness[18] is negated here.

iii. **Essential Approach is not Enough**

Here the postulate is: the one universal religion. The different existing religions can be explained analogically. As there is only one human nature, so also there is only one nature for the different religions. In short, as it is possible to have only one concept of religion, there can be only one religion[19] and one theological methodology. The essential approach can give rise to two different attitudes:

a) that of the maximalists: The only one religion is ours. The other so-called religions are false, or are only religious appearance. Artificial silver is not real silver.[20] This approach gives rise to the „heteronomic" attitude--the superiority and dominance of one religion over the other.[21] Heteronomy is a world view and also „an anthropological degree of consciousness, which relies on a hierarchical structure of reality, which considers that the regulations in any sphere of being come from a higher instance, and are in each case responsible, so to speak, for the proper functioning of that particular being or sphere of being."[22] Heteronomical world view splits sacred and profane too sharply and profane is viewed under the authoritarian subjugation of God.[23]

b) That of the minimalists: There is only one RELIGION, whose nature is reflected in other existing religions. The nature of this RELIGION is the real nature of religions; not that only one religion is true, but that RELIGION is true. The different religions are less fulfilled embodiments of the common nature of RELIGION.[24]

In the essential approach there is a preoccupation with monolithic or totalitarian uniformity.[25] Such a uniformity paves the way either for exclusivism, fanaticism and intolerance;[26] or for inclusivism, eclectism, syncretism, producing indifference.[27] So a purely essential approach cannot realistically take into consideration the plurality of religions. Therefore, it cannot be admissible for theologizing in the context of world religions.

iv. Existential Approach is Inadequate

One must not go on abstracting and reaching an unreal essence of religions. The existing religions are there because they are somehow useful for humanity. Instead of envisaging a common essence of all religions, let us try to solve the theological problems of individual religions.[28]

Neither the `essential` nor the `existential' approach is admissible.[29] Religion is neither a simple essence, nor is it, in its full, existence. It is a complex human endeavour in which God and the cosmos are circumscribed. But at the same time, it is adapted to the present form of human person in pilgrimage.[30]

v. Doctrinal Comparison is Insufficient

One may perhaps compare the Hindu and Christian ideas of grace. Perhaps both may meet at certain points. Yet essentially, they are different, since one is the doctrine of a Hindu and the other of a Christian.[31] „They would be the same intellectual garb for different historical realities."[32]

After studying a doctrine dialectically, perhaps one may find one doctrine better than the other. Yet the weaker doctrine cannot be given up by its upholder, „because it is deeply rooted in the core of his own religion, which he holds from supra- and/or extra-rational motives.... Even dialectics have their limits: in the undeniable existence of the other as a source of self-understanding and in the non-rational factors that play a role in our convictions."[33] Theories belong only to an intermediate stage between the existential foundation of a supra-rational faith and the ethical consequence of practical life. The real encounter in fact takes place at a much deeper level.[34]

There is more scope for the mystical approach „than for merely doctrinal discussion, for exclusively conceptual thinking." In stating this Panikkar is not „underestimating the importance of theoretical studies. It is sometimes only too easy to rely on (existential or mystical) 'experience', while ignoring the far-reaching theoretical implications of every existential attitude. The praxis requires a theory and the theory has to lead to a praxis."[35]

vi. The Trinitarian, the *Advaitic* Middle Way

Panikkar proposes as a hermeneutical principle 'pluralism'. This pluralism is between an Unrelated Plurality and a Monolithic Unity.[36] A non-dualistic attitude (pluralism) in the face of plurality is one of the main presuppositions of the methodology of Panikkar.[37] Human life is complex. It has a plurality of faculties and manifold functions. „The human being is not a single entity but a set of relations. All that is in us and around us seems to be manifold. We live under the sign of multiplicity, and human civilization tends to further multiply knowledge, distinctions, methods. And life itself: there seems to be a natural dynamism toward complexity..."[38] We must accept this pluralism as the real growth of humanity instead of reducing all things into a single system or empire. The tower of Babel is a warning against constructing any monolithic conception of reality.[39] In order to theologize in the context of the multiplicity of religions one must take pluralism as a hermeneutical principle.

The pluralistic age finds a place for everything. The overemphasis on the separation between sacred and secular is not valid. This can be the reason for the secularizing tendency of the world religions.[40] „The whole of reality cannot be reduced to one single principle. In spite of all the subtle ontological distinctions on the ultimate level, a single principle would necessarily consume all the rest. There has also to be dynamism and a certain type of pluralism within the highest unity. Contrariwise, reality cannot be sheer unrelated plurality either. In spite of all the differences and irreducibilities; the very awareness of plurality entails a higher unity. There has also to be a certain relationship between the ultimate ingredients of reality. This is, I submit, what the doctrine of the Trinity as well as that of Advaita stand for."[41] In Hinduism the paradigm for this mystery is the *Advaitic* intuition, „which refers to something which cannot be called either 'one' or `two'. The Mystery towards which the religious experience of Humankind tends is neither the same nor different, neither one nor many: it is non-dualistic."[42] The ultimate reality is neither pure dichotomies nor totally blurred distinctions. „The advaitic character of reality does not permit ultimate dichotomies between matter and spirit, thinker and thought, creator and created, and the like. Nor does it blur the distinctions. On the contrary, it underlines them: the three worlds of the divine, the cosmic, and the human are differentiated, but not separated; they are three real dimensions of the one and the same reality, and it is precisely this three dimensionality, as it were, which makes reality one." The four *mahāvākyas* call for a theanthropocosmic, „of discovering the whole of reality and finding in it the role of Man.... The drama is not only a display of the One, but also its `play' in order that the many may become and may realize oneness."[43]

Advaita is for a full and uncompromising Oneness, and makes room for pluralism. In the advaitic vision, reality is neither a monistic block nor a metaphysical apartheid.[44]

a. Pluralism: The Others from Their Own Point of View

The effort is made „to overcome unconnected plurality without, however, falling into undifferentiated unity."[45] One cannot and must not reduce „the pluralistic variety of Man into one single religion, system, ideology or tradition." It is in these actual polarities of our human existence that we find our real being.[46]

Pluralism „begins with the recognition of otherness, which already implies my sameness. I am in relation."[47] It is based on trust in the other.[48] Otherness is not the other. The other „does not see himself as other, but as *ego*, as I myself see myself. To have treated the other as otherness instead of an *alius*, to have reified the other and not to have allowed him a place in my-self, is one of the greatest confusions the human being can fall into." It is said: love the other as oneself. „There can be no true pluralism until the other is discovered. I mean the other (*alius*) as a source of (self) understanding and not only as a term (*aliud*) of intelligibility."[49] When we turn to the other without our pre-conceived ideas or without our self-assertion[50] about the other, we are trying to find the whole person. This turning is to understand the other in his own terms. This will help us with what we really do not understand.[51] The question is „whether I can grasp what he thinks about himself."[52] We must not think that we possess „the philosophers' stone" and know everything about the other, about other systems. „This is not irrationalism. It is intellectual humility or common sense." If we can learn with this humility „not to think through everything", we will save „the `thought' (*das Gedachte, not der Gedanke*) and the thinker."[53]

Pluralism „does not stem from the *logos*, but from the *mythos*. Pluralism is grounded in the belief that no single group embraces the totality of human experience."[54] „No religion, ideology...can reasonably claim to exhaust the universal range of human experience. Thus a *pluralism* distinct from the mere coexistence of a plurality of worldviews is a present-day necessity."[55] There is "almost a mythical confidence that other perspectives may also be plausible."[56]

In this plurality seeking understanding, „Dialogical philosophy" can be useful. Rather than comparison between philosophies or philosophers it is a process a multi-voiced philosophy in which the different problems are allowed to express themselves according to their own categories, contexts and self-understandings. It is no longer a question of the scientific way of understanding how elements function so much as knowing what they are.[57] Thus „Pluralism testifies that one has passed beyond *absolutism*, without thereby tumbling into agnostic *relativism.* Pluralism presupposes only a radical *relativity* underlying all human constructs and at the bottom of reality itself."[58]

b. Need of Diatopical Hermeneutics: Morphological and Diachronical, is not enough

In the awareness of pluralism, only a diatopical hermeneutics will be adequate. One could distinguish a threefold hermeneutics as „three intertwined ways of overcoming the epistemological distance and thus the human estrangement."[59] Morphological hermeneutics tries to decipher, to explain the values of one's own culture to the same cultural community. Here one logically unfolds what is implicit or *de facto* unknown elements.[60] It is rather like a youngster trying to learn about the past from contemporaries.[61] Diachronical hermeneutics shows that text and context are intimately related, so that to understand a text the knowledge of the context is necessary. The „temporal gap between the understander and that which is to be understood" may obscure or even change the meaning of the original datum. So, the temporal factor is an intrinsic element in the process of understanding. It is a movement from the present to the past in order to incorporate, subsume or delete it. It is like an adult who, having a conviction about the present, tries also to enrich himself by understanding the past. The method is fundamentally historical.[62] These two hermeneutics have been applied in theology. But when we encounter a totally different culture or religious tradition, the above two hermeneutics turn insufficient, hence the major causes of misunderstanding between cultures. Here it is a question not only of a temporal gap between text and context in the same tradition, but both the text and the context are different.

In order to face this situation Panikkar proposes Diatopical hermeneutics. The gap is between two human *topoi*, 'places' of understanding. This is between cultures that have not developed their patterns of intelligibility or basic assumptions out of a common tradition. „To cross the boundaries of one's own culture without realizing that another culture may have a radically different approach to reality is today no longer admissible.... Diatopical hermeneutics stands for the thematic consideration of understanding the other without assuming that the other has the same basic self-understanding and understanding as I have."[63] Not only contexts, but also the very myth, the ultimate human horizon, is at stake here. So, logical or historical method is not enough. A transhistorical, translogical method is necessary, „a peculiar dialogical dialogue, dìa-lógos piercing the logos". Then we will reach the translogical realm of the heart, enabling us to enter into the other's myth, the horizon of intelligibility. This entering will not consider the other's myth as object of study, but as source of original self-understanding.[64] Then plurality will not be a source of threat but a rich source for communion.

c. Plurality, not unrelatedness, but unity

Plurality is not Sheer Unrelatedness, but Unity Keeping Plurality as in the case of Ultimate Reality. The monistic reductionism must be avoided. Monists believe that the structure of the world is simple. If at all there is complexity, it is because of the unfolding of this single source. This monistic attitude has a pessimism concerning the secondary structures of reality. This „attitude reposes on a monotheistic belief in a perfect, and thus simple, God at the very source of reality. To return to that source is the meaning of life."[65]

There must be a perception of the „dynamism and a certain type of pluralism within the highest unity." At the same time, „reality cannot be sheer unrelated plurality either. In spite of all the differences and irreducibilities, the very awareness of plurality entails a higher unity. There has also to be a certain relationship between the ultimate ingredients of reality."[66] This is expressed by some philosophical thought about and religious experiences of the ultimate reality. „According to Parmenides reality is given in the now as totality (*pān*), oneness (*hen*), and complexity (*syneches*).... This is probably the language of most mystics...."[67] Nicholas of Cusa presents God as the „*complexio omnium*". Teilhard de Chardin „sees the evolution of the universe toward an increasing complexity."[68] This vision of complexity and higher unity in the ultimate reality is what Panikkar himself expressed by the „cosmotheandric character of reality".[69] „The underlying myths for the doctrines of the Trinity"[70] and nondualism, Advaita, and many other myths, might stand for this insight.[71]

[1] Panikkar, „The Internal Dialogue:...," *Religion and Society* Vol. XV, No.3 (September 1968), pp. 65-66.

[2]R. Panikkar, *Salvation in Christ:...*, (1972), p. 79. „If Christian experience is to open itself up to cultures different from those in which it has been couched, it has to be still more open to world-views...." Panikkar, *Salvation in Christ:...*, (1972), p. 73.

[3]Panikkar, *Salvation in Christ:...*, (1972), pp. 78-79.

[4] E. Cousins, „...Panikkar Symposium...," *Cross Currents*, (Summer 1979), p. 133.

[5]E. Cousins, „...Panikkar Symposium...," *Cross Currents*, (Summer 1979), p. 133. .

[6] Panikkar, „Metatheology...," *Concilium*, (June 1969), p. 26.

[7] E. Cousins, „...Panikkar Symposium...," *Cross Currents*, (Summer 1979), pp. 132-133.

[8] E. Cousins, „Raimundo Panikkar and the Christian systematic theology of the future," *Cross Currents* 29 (Summer 1979), p. 143.

[9] E. Cousins, „...Theology of the future," *Cross Currents*, 29 (Summer 1979), pp. 151-152.

[10] Panikkar, *The Trinity...*, [1970] (1973), p. 59.

[11] Panikkar, *The Unknown...*, (1981), p. 22. cf. also p. 21.

[12] W. Capps, „Toward a Christian theology of the World's Religions," *Cross Currents* 29 (Summer 1979), pp. 168, 182.

[13]E. Cousins, „...Panikkar Symposium...," *Cross Currents*, (Summer 1979), p. 133.

[14]Panikkar, *Religionen....*, [1964] (1965), pp. 21-24.

[15]Panikkar, *Religionen....*, [1964] (1965), pp. 19-21.

[16]Panikkar, „Philosophy of Religion in the Contemporary Encounter of Cultures." in R. Klibansky, ed., *Contemporary Philosophy: A Survey*, (Firenze: La Nuova Editrice, 1971), p. 234.

[17] Panikkar, *Worship and Secular Man: An essay on the liturgical nature of Man, considering Secularization as a major phenomenon of our time and worship as an apparent fact of all times: A study towards an integral Anthropology*, (London: Darton, Longman and Todd; and New York: Orbis Books, 1973), p. 28, cf. also pp. 37-38. Cf., also Panikkar,

Kultmysterium...., (1964), pp. 81-83.

[18]Panikkar, „Philosophy of Religion...," in R. Klibansky, ed., *Contemporary Philosophy: A Survey*, (1971), p. 222.

[19]„Das essentielle Denken wird betonen, da$ es nur eine Religion gibt, weil es nur einen Begriff `Religion' gibt." Panikkar, *Religionen....*, [1964] (1965), p. 27.

[20]Panikkar, *Religionen....*, [1964] (1965), p. 27.

[21]Panikkar, „Philosophy of Religion...," in R. Klibansky, ed., *Contemporary Philosophy: A Survey*, (1971), p. 234.

[22] Panikkar, *Worship...*, (1973), p. 28

[23] Cf. Panikkar, *Worship...*, (1973), pp. 30, 32, 34. Cf. also Panikkar, *Kultmysterium....*, (1964), pp. 78-81.

[24]Panikkar, *Religionen....*, [1964] (1965), p. 27.

[25]Panikkar, *Religionen....*, [1964] (1965), p. 14; cf. pp. 149-150. Cf. Panikkar, *Kerygma und Indien....*, (1967), p. 15.

[26]Cf. Panikkar, *Religionen....*, [1964] (1965), p. 11.

[27]Panikkar, *Religionen....*, [1964] (1965), pp. 14, 11; also cf. Panikkar, „Response to Harold Coward," *Cross Currents* 29 (Summer 1979), p. 191.

[28]Panikkar, *Religionen....*, [1964] (1965), p. 27.

[29]Panikkar, *The Unknown...*, (1981), p. 22.

[30]„Die Religion ist nicht einfach ihr Wesen, noch eine vollkommene Existenz. Sie ist eine komplexe menschliche Tatsache, die Gott und den Kosmos umschließt, aber der zeitlichen Form unseres pilgernden Seins angepaßt ist." Panikkar, *Religionen....*, [1964] (1965), p. 28.

[31]Panikkar, *The Unknown....*, (1981), p. 40.

[32]Panikkar, *The Unknown....*, (1981), p. 40.

[33]Panikkar, *The Unknown....*, (1981), p. 40. „Since many a philosophy or religion regards itself as ultimate, we cannot justifiably compare that which purports to be unique and uncomparable. For this reason I prefer the neologism, ImparativePhilosophy, since we can only truly *imparare*,

learn by being ready to undergo the different experiences of other peoples, philosophies and religions. This kind of learning is reflective, critical and provisional." Panikkar, „Hermeneutics ...Religion:..," *The Journal of Religious Studies* VI, (Spring 1978), p. 45.

[34]Panikkar *The Unknown....*, (1964), pp. 8-9.

[35]Panikkar, *The Unknown....*, (1981), p. 40.

[36]„Pluralism stands between unrelated plurality and a monolithic unity." Panikkar, *The Intrareligious Dialogue*, (1978), p. xxvii. Cf. also Panikkar „Die Säckularisierung der Hermeneutik. Der Fall Christus: Menschensohn und Gottessohn," [1976] in *Kerygma und Mythos VI - 9: zum problem der Sékularisierung ; Mythos oder Wirklichkeit Verhängnis oder Verhei$ung?* E. Grassi, P. Ricoeur and others (Hamburg: Bergstedt, H. Reich 1977), p. 143. Cf. Panikkar, „The Threefold Linguistic Intrasubjectivity," Archivio di Filosofia LIV, no., 1-3, (1986), p. 606.

[37]Panikkar uses pluralism as a modern secular word for the `non-dualism'. Cf. Panikkar, *The Unknown...*, (1981), pp. 23-24.

[38]Panikkar, *Blessed Simplicity: The Monk as Universal Archetype*, (New York: Seabury Press, 1982), p. 29.

[39]Panikkar, „The Myth of Pluralism: The Tower of Babel - A Meditation on Non-Violence," *Cross-Currents* 29, (Summer, 1979), pp. 197-200; cf. p. 216.

[40]Cf. R. Panikkar, *The Trinity...*, [1970] (1973), p. 58.

[41]R. Panikkar, *Blessed Simplicity:...*, (1982), p. 38. Cf. Panikkar „Die Säkularisierung...," [1976] in *Kerygma und Mythos* VI - 9, (1977), pp. 142 n. 2; 161.

[42] Panikkar, The Unknown..., (1981), pp. 23 24.

[43] Panikkar, The Vedic Experience:...., [1977] (1979), pp. 658-659.

[44]Panikkar, <u>The Vedic Experience</u>:..., [1977] (1979), pp. 657-658.

[45]Panikkar, „Hermeneutics ...Religion:..," *The Journal of Religious Studies* VI, (Spring 1978), p. 45.

[46]Panikkar, *The Intrareligious Dialogue*, (1978), pp. xxvii-xxviii.

[47]Panikkar, „The Myth of Pluralism...," *Cross Currents*, 29 (Summer 1979), p. 217.

[48]Panikkar, „ Śunaḥśepa. A Myth of the Human Condition," [1974] *Myth, Faith and Hermeneutics*:..., (1979), p. 102.

[49]Panikkar, „The Myth of Pluralism...," *Cross Currents*, 29 (Summer 1979), pp. 217-218.

[50]Panikkar, „Hermeneutics ...Religion:..," *The Journal of Religious Studies* VI, (Spring 1978), p. 45.

[51]Panikkar, „Hermeneutics ...Religion:..," *The Journal of Religious Studies* VI, (Spring 1978), p. 44. Cf. Panikkar, „Metatheology...," *Concilium*, (June 1969), pp. 26-27. Cf. Panikkar, „The Hermeneutics of Hermeneutics...," [1963] *Philosophy Today* 2 (Fall 1967), p. 179.

[52]Panikkar, „Hermeneutics ...Religion:..," *The Journal of Religious Studies* VI, (Spring 1978), p. 45.

[53]Panikkar, „The Myth of Pluralism...," *Cross Currents*, 29 (Summer 1979), pp. 224-225.

[54]„...pluralism bears witness that one has transcended the <u>logos</u> as sole and final arbiter of the real, though without belittling its sway." Panikkar, „ Śunaḥśepa...," [1974] *Myth, Faith and Hermeneutics*:..., (1979), p. 102.

[55] Panikkar, „...Monopoly on Religion?" *Journal of Ecumenical Studies*, 11 (Summer 1974), p. 516.

[56]Panikkar, „...Monopoly on Religion?" *Journal of Ecumenical Studies*, 11 (Summer 1974), p. 516.

[57]Panikkar, „Hermeneutics ...Religion:..," *The Journal of Religious Studies* VI (Spring 1978), p. 45.

[58]Panikkar, „ Śunaḥśepa....," [1974] *Myth, Faith and Hermeneutics:...,* (1979), p. 102. „The problem of pluralism arises...because the very nature of reality is pluralistic." Panikkar, „The Myth of Pluralism...," *Cross Currents,* 29 (Summer 1979), p. 216.

[59]Panikkar, *Myth, Faith and Hermeneutics:...,* (1979), p. 8.

[60]Cf. Panikkar, *Myth, Faith and Hermeneutics:...,* (1979), p. 8.

[61]Panikkar, *Myth, Faith and Hermeneutics:...,* (1979), p. 9.

[62]Cf. Panikkar, *Myth, Faith and Hermeneutics:...,* (1979), pp. 8-9.

[63]Panikkar, *Myth, Faith and Hermeneutics:...,* (1979), p. 9.

[64]Panikkar, *Myth, Faith and Hermeneutics:...,* (1979), pp. 9-10.

[65] Panikkar, *Blessed Simplicity...,* (1982), pp. 36-37, cf. pp. 38

[66]Panikkar, *Blessed Simplicity...,* (1982), pp. 38.

[67]Panikkar, *Blessed Simplicity...,* (1982), p. 39.

[68]Panikkar, *Blessed Simplicity...,* (1982), pp. 35-36.

[69]Panikkar, *Blessed Simplicity...,* (1982), p. 38.

[70]Panikkar, „The Myth of Pluralism...," *Cross Currents,* 29 (Summer 1979), p. 216. Cf. Panikkar, *Blessed Simplicity...,* (1982), pp. 38, 128.

[71]R. Panikkar, „The Myth of Pluralism...," *Cross Currents,* 29 (Summer 1979), p. 216. Cf. R. Panikkar, *Blessed Simplicity...,* (1982),pp. 38, 129.

VII

The Helical Movement towards Metatheology

As mentioned above, the proper method for theologizing in the context of world religions is not centrifugalism, centripetalism, or an „essential or existential" approach; not by autonomic[1] or heteronomic[2] attitudes, but by an approach of synthesis[3] achieved by the helical movement[4] with an ontonomic attitude--basic interrelationship of all religions.[5]

A. Ontonomic attitude

Ontonomy is a degree of awareness. According to Panikkar, having overcome the individualistic attitude and the monolithic view of reality, it „regards the whole universe as unity so that the regulation of a particular being is neither self-imposed nor dictated from above, but a part of the whole discovering or following its destiny. Ontonomy is the realization of the *nomos*, the law of the *on*, being, at that profound level where unity does not impinge upon diversity, but where the latter is rather the unique and proper manifestation of the former. It rests on the *specular* character of reality, in which each `part' mirrors the whole in a way proper to it."[6] Ontonomy perceives each aspect of a being or universe in the light of the whole. The whole is neither different nor identical with one of its different fields of being. The whole reality of the universe has „an internal and constitutive relationship between all and every part of reality".[7]

A. **Synthesis through helix**

The all-embracing synthesis is through the helix. This helix has a centre and a law of growth; it not only has contact with all spheres of human life but also touches all existent religions of the world, faithful to real human historical concreteness.[8] Whatever differences in the humanity, all can experience as one as humankind.[9] This can be applied in the context of world religions.

The basic factor is that theology in the context of the world religions and other cultures demands a radical examination of conscience in the face of this new situation. There may come a radical awareness that every religion is one's neighbour, and every neighbour one's brother. „God is that which makes it possible to discover my brother in my neighbor."[10] This spiral method is not merely a return either to Hindu doctrines alone nor to Christian teaching alone. It is a going forward for a new creation allowing the religious traditions mutual indwelling, „circumincessio"[11]

True to the model 'circumincessio,' Theology of religion would not reduce all diversities, human and religious, to one uniform common denominator. It would allow to grow within its field the most variegated forms of beliefs and religious traditions, overcoming resentment, envy, isolationism and misunderstandings by making room for a healthy and natural pluralism. It is not by putting all on one plate we are going to have a true theology of religion, but by discovering the religious root of human, which grows up until it flourishes and gives fruit in the most multiform way. The religions will not be private properties constricted in the walls of enclosures, but open garden for all. Such a theology is possible the mystical experience of the truth from within of all religious tradition.[12]

As the epochs of 'political Christianity,' of 'Empires,' of 'Colonialism,' are past, there is a better situation now to understand other religions from the interior. The encounter of religions is taking place at the round table of world couture on an equal footing. There is more possibility of theological 'pluralism' with a multiplicity of hermeneutics.[13] For that, as in the helix, there must be a move spirally in space and time: forward and upward. As a result, there comes about a real existential catholicity, a true universality as the fullness and dynamic point of convergence of all religious denominations.[14] „By collaborating towards universalization of Christianity, towards the *actualization* in fact of its catholicity, one is contributing to the development of all religions towards unity...."[15]

i. Metatheology

The need of the time is metatheology. Theology cannot remain restricted to a particular group if it takes seriously the Catholicity of Christianity and also seeks to be relevant to other world views. It must take into „account the contemporary situation, keeping loyalty to Christian tradition without betraying other streams of mankind's religious experience."[16]

Humanity is trying to appropriate symbols transcending national, racial, cultural and geographical boundaries. For instance, there can be doubts whether in the planetarian horizon, the american flag planted in moon appropriately symbolized to represent the leap of humanity. Similarly, there are considerations to examine whether, in the multi-religious context, will the conception of a personal God express the fullness of the mystery of God.[17] Finding the relativity of language the Christian theology must transcend an intra-cultural discourse to face up the globalization of not only political and economic, but also intellectual, cultural and religious problems.[18]

The call for universality of theology can be sensed here.[19] For this we may need to reformulate the preambles of our fundamental theology. Together with the human person and the Church, the latter's dogmatic formulations are on a pilgrimage. As the humanity, together with their cultures, religions, and the church are in pilgrimage towards heavenly Jerusalem, the theology is also provisional, the dogmas were and is on a pilgrimage for further explication and enrichment.[20] Panikkar writes, „....the range of human experience, subjective and objective, has radically changed since the times in which the Christian doctrine was formulated and can no longer be identified with the Christian context."[21] Because of the change of world views and differing cultural, geographical and religious backgrounds, our commonly held assumptions and presuppositions are undergoing a crisis.[22] Many African languages, for instance, are struggling to find appropriate words for the concepts of nature and person, which are completely foreign to the consciousness of the peoples. This situation need not be considered as a problem for Christian preaching in Africa. It could lead to an enrichment and rejuvenation of the central dogma of Christianity for the theology of tomorrow.[23]

Similarly, for instance, the preambles of fundamental theology cannot be valid in some of the world religions and secular movements. Buddhism has no God and, for the 'death of God theology,' God is outdated. How can we do theology in a way relevant for these situations too? Is 'God talk' really essential to religious experience? Does not 'God talk' arise because of particular religious, philosophical and cultural contexts? There is a task awaiting theology of proving that the Christian message may become meaningful in any authentic human attitude and genuine philosophical position; that the Christian *kerygma* is not, in principle, tied down to any philosophical system or cultural scheme--not even to any religious tradition. For instance, theology has a duty to explain that not only does the acceptance of the existence of God is a necessary pre-requisite to understand and accept Christian faith, but also that, under the hypothesis of there being no God, if this is existentially given, the Christian proclamation could look for a justification and a meaning.[24]

In this situation, the role of fundamental theology would be to work out the intelligibility of theology also outside the culture and even the religion where that theology has until now grown and prospered. Fundamental theology, sometimes, has to grow beyond or even shed its past. „Fundamental theology is an Exodus theology." And it is very urgent. „Today two-thirds of the world population live in a non-historical dimension; half of mankind does not have the theistic conception of God as the Children of Abraham have...one-third of human beings lack a consciousness of separated individuality.... In a word, the function of fundamental theology consists in providing a theological justification of a theological as well as a religious pluralism."[25]

Such a theology is possible. Even though Buddhists do not believe in God, they would like to believe in the whole message of Christ and sincerely think that they could accept it and even understand it better if it could be purified from what they consider to be its theistic superstructure. Hindus have no problem as far as the Resurrected Christ is concerned. But they will wonder why they have to join a physical and cultural community only because of their belief in the divinity of Christ and in his Resurrection. The secularist theologian, though a Christian, accepts neither God nor the Resurrection as they are traditionally understood. „The 'Death of God' theologian...will say it is precisely because Christ is the saviour that he can dispense with any conception of a transcendent God or a physical miracle." Can we call these three types Christian?[26]

Metatheology is not just another system of theology, just as metaphysics is not simply a more refined physical science. A theological system may still be theistic; metatheology does not need to be so and may be, for instance, at the origin of a non-theistic theological reflection. Still, it is a theological investigation. Fundamental theology tries to understand the fundamental theological issue (Christ, for the Christian faith) in a given philosophical, religious and cultural situation.[27] However, according to Panikkar: „It is methodologically wrong to start, for instance, by saying that the stumbling-block for a Christian-Hindu dialogue is the denial of the personal character of the divine; as it is equally inaccurate to say at the outset that unless one reaches the level of an all-pervading attributeless Brahman (considered as the highest possible religious awareness) there is no possible encounter of Hinduism with the other world religions."[28]

The presence of other religions will help to reach the fundamentals of Christianity. „In one word, '*das Ungedachte*', the unthought, can be disclosed only by him who does not 'think' like me: he helps me to discover the unthought *magma* out of which my thinking crystallizes, and I on my part can do him the same service."[29] Therefore, the „faith of the enlightened Christian must strip itself of the `christian religion' as it actually exists and free itself for a fecundation that will affect all religions both ancient and modern."[30]

The situation is almost the same as in the past when Christian theology encountered the Greek philosophy. The intention of Panikkar is not a mere adaptation of occidental (Western) thinking. Panikkar intends to discover Christ with a thinking beginning from Hinduism, with a Hindu-Christian theology without leaving Christ as the monopoly of Mediterranean, Jewish, Hellenistic, Latin, Celtic, Gothic thinking.[31] The error consists in trying to equate the Christian mystery with the expression present in one of these particular frames of reference.[32] Panikkar wants to follow the initiative taken in the patristic period by Justin and Clement of Alexandria,[33] and continued through St Thomas Aquinas.[34]

St Thomas, while taking up Hellenistic thinking, that of Aristotle in particular, „was undertaking a theological mission of assimilation, namely, an explanation of Christian truths by adoption of the Aristotelian framework conveniently transformed. He was not concerned with aseptic `scientific' hermeneutics, but sought only the truth."[35] But seeking the fulness of truth through the Aristotelian categories has a double effect: It explicates further the fulness of the truth in Christian faith and also explicates what Aristotle really wanted to say.[36] We can take the same approach in the Hindu religious and philosophical context. We must „turn to the possible understanding of this classical Christian tenet from a perspective that has in view other religious traditions."[37]

Cousins states that Christian systematic theology having remained within the Western culture and its intellectual history, it remains uninfluenced and unenriched by the world religions. There is an urgent need for Christian systematic theology to encompass within its horizons the religious experience of mankind by encountering of world religions.[38] Cousins urges that the global religious experience must be related to all the central Christian doctrines--not merely to salvation history. The Christian doctrines of the Trinity, of Christ, and of redemption must be explored in such a way that they will be open to, in relation with, and enriched by, the religious experience of humankind. This must be done not remaining only in the Christian *Weltanschauung*, and looking upon all other religions as falling into a similar category. Christian theologians „must reach out and enter into the very subjectivity of the other traditions in their distinct variety, and must bring this into the structure of a systematic theology."[39]

Perhaps the deep intuitions of Hinduism and Buddhism, which come from a different universe of discourse than the Greek, may help us penetrate further the Trinitarian mystery. Panikkar states: „After all, is not theology precisely the endeavour of the man of faith to express his religious experience in the mental and cultural context in which he is situated?"[40] If we take the philosophy of Śaṅkara and Rāmānuja, for example, we may get a profound insight into the problem of Nature and Person in the Trinity and Christology. It will be as important as a theologian of the first century had discovered the philosophy of Plato and Aristotle in the Middle Ages.[41] Reciprocally, we may get a clear awareness of what Śaṅkara and Rāmānuja were intending to say while they were struggling with the problem of the relation between Brahman, *Īśvara* and the world.

ii. **Christology in the Context of Religions, Metatheology**

Christology, in the context of the theology of religion, must also take on the metatheological dimension. The major theological problem of finding „an adequate theology of religion, capable of encompassing the whole range of man's religious experience today"[42] must be reflected in contemporary Christological thinking. The inspiration and motive force for this task is the „critical understanding of the Christian dynamism of `establishing all things in Christ' (Eph. 1:10)."[43] To make the phenomenon of Jesus important for the entire world, it must not be treated exclusively in one system of thinking. „In today's world not only no single tradition and religion is self-sufficient, but also no single method is appropriate for approaching the fact of Jesus. We cannot do justice to the significance of Christ for the present and coming generations without integrating other experiences and ways of intelligibility within the Christian culture and outside it."[44] Then the proper task of fundamental theology as a separate discipline is not to defend *a priori* „a particular philosophy as more adequate than another for explaining Christian belief, but to have such a deep and, I would add, mystical experience of Jesus, that one may express it in whatever cultural tools one may have at his disposal."[45] The question is „whether it is at all possible to accept Jesus in a non-semitic way which at the same time may not be considered unacceptable for the Jewish-Christian mentality."[46] This is, for example, one of the capital and agonizing problems which the so-called young churches of Africa and Asia are facing.[47] Perhaps we have to reconsider whether we have to mention the Greek name of Christ in order to have a Christocentric nature of the theology of religions.[48] „Today we are critically aware that the Christian *a priori* of Christ being the unique Mediator and Christianity the true religion is embedded in time, space, culture and a particular human understanding....Any Christian reflection today must reconsider its starting-point and, at the least, justify it in the human arena."[49] The concern is „to indicate an understanding of Jesus according to Christian Scripture and human contemporary Tradition, an attempt to explore one of the central problems of `fundamental theology': the awareness of a cosmotheandric principle, of an incarnated *mandalic* center, which could become one of the bases for a `theology of religion'...."[50]

Felipe Gomes has his reservations about Panikkar's attempt of assimilating elements from the teachings ofBuddha, Krishna and the like into Christology for, the uniqueness of Christ, which is the greatest 'stumbling block,' will be erased.[51] Panikkar's intention is not to „dilute the Christian message or evade the `folly of the Cross' or avoid the Christian `scandal'. To use the latter as an excuse for condemning others or to stick stubbornly to one's own ideas is not exactly Christian scandal.... On the contrary, I maintained that to pretend to an exhaustive knowledge of the mystery of Christ is to empty the Cross of its power."[52]

The real stumbling block in the process of interaction with the world religions is not Jesus Christ. It is how contemporary Christianity presents Jesus Christ. For instance, one extreme far right form was presenting Christ as a mere divine idol; at the same time, a far left movement was also there, presenting Jesus as just a revolutionary Jew.[53]

Therefore, it is necessary to deepen the Christian understanding of the Mystery of Christ especially by experience. It will help to present the real Jesus Christ,[54] in a way that makes sense to other religions. Christology speaking about Christ in inter-religious context will help solve, for instance, „philosophical misunderstandings about Christ and the incarnation, from the side of Indian philosophy".[55]

It is this vision that we find in some of Panikkar's important works: *The Unknown Christ of Hinduism,*[56]*Salvation in Christ: Concreteness and Universality; The Supername;*[57]*The Trinity and World Religions: Icon-Person-Mystery*[58] and others. Even though he has not developed a thorough system in Christology, it „has been a continuing concern of Panikkar.... This is not surprising since Christology is the critical area of any ecumenical theology."[59] He tries to articulate who Christ is in the world religious context. The special feature of

Panikkar's Christological statements is that he writes not only as a Christian but also as a scholar of comparative religions who has himself been exposed to the various world religions,[60] especially Hinduism, on the common platform of interreligious dialogue. His continued effort is to examine his own Christian faith, and the deeper dimensions of the mystery of Christ, not only in the pursuit of a possible union between religions but also for intra-religious theologising, enriched by inter-religious dialogue. [61]

As the scope of the present book is to present the fundamentals to understand Panikkar's thought, in the forthcoming books of the series *Panikkar's Christological prayāṇa*, the Christologial contributions of Panikkar will be worked out.

[1]Autonomy: the thinking that „each field is absolutely self-normative and patron of its own destiny." Panikkar, *Worship*..., (1973), p. 41.

[2]Heteronomy: „The regulation of the activity of a particular being by laws proceeding from another higher being." Panikkar, *Worship*..., (1973), p. 41.

[3]Cf. Panikkar, *Religionen*....., [1964] (1965), p. 11.

[4]Panikkar, *Religionen*....., [1964] (1965), p. 150.

[5]R. Panikkar, „Philosophy of Religion...," in R. Klibansky, ed., *Contemporary Philosophy: A Survey*, (1971), p. 234.

[6] Panikkar, *Worship*..., (1973), p. 29.

[7]„Ontonomy is intended to express the recognition of the inner regularities of each field of activity or sphere of being in the light of the whole. The whole is, in fact, neither different from nor merely identical with any one field or sphere. Ontonomy rests on the assumption that the universe is a whole, that there is an internal and

constitutive relationship between all and every part of reality, that nothing is disconnected and that the development and progress of one being is not to be at the expense of another--not because it should or ought not, but for the same reason adduced in the case of cancer, namely that neither promotes the life of the whole organism nor is of any utility for the affected organ." Panikkar, *Worship...*, (1973), p. 42. Cf., also Panikkar, *Kultmysterium....*, (1964), pp. 83-86.

[8]Panikkar, *Religionen....*, [1964] (1965), p. 150. We have to experience the gathering or concentrating in ourselves „more than one of the human phyla in which mankind's fundamental insights have accumulated. We want to be no longer sons of Manu or Israel or Ishmael alone, but children of Man.

„The different traits here taken into account are brought together to form a tress which represents one of the deepest intuitions man has had and is still having, from different points of view and with different names:...." Panikkar, *The Trinity...*, [1970] (1973), pp. x-xi.

[9] We have to experience the gathering or concentrating in ourselves „more than one of the human phyla in which mankind's fundamental insights have accumulated. We want to be no longer sons of Manu or Israel or Ishmael alone, but children of Man.

„The different traits here taken into account are brought together to form a tress which represents one of the deepest intuitions man has had and is still having, from different points of view and with different names:...." Panikkar, *The Trinity...*, [1970] (1973), pp. x-xi.

[10]Panikkar, „Philosophy of Religion...," in R. Klibansky, ed., Contemporary Philosophy: A Survey, (1971), p. 239.

[11]„The <u>circumincessio</u> (and here I am uttering something which may be debatable to people who see tradition only as guarding the past, not trying to discover that tradition is to take and to pass on, thus looking towards the future)--is not well represented by circle, for it is not going back to the origins, it is new creation. The spiral may perhaps be a more appropriate--but the spiral on three-dimensional levels where the point is still being created by the very fact that you go another circle--so the paradox is this <u>circumincessio</u> in its spiral mode between being and non-being, not that one just goes back to the origins." Panikkar, „The Silence of the Word: Non-dualistic Polarities," [in `Discussion'], [1970] *Cross Currents*, (Summer/Fall 1974), p. 171.

[12]Panikkar, „The Internal Dialogue:..," *Religion and Society* Vol. XV, (September 1968), pp. 65-66. „One of the most characteristic phenomena of our age is undoubtedly the encounter of religions. It is happening today, perhaps for the first time, at the round table of world culture on an equal footing. The epochs of 'political Christianity,' of 'Empires,' of 'Colonialism,' are past and we find ourselves better situated today to understand other religions from the interior. All that leads us to a qualified acceptance and elaboration of even theological 'pluralism,' or, in other words, of the basic possiblity of a multiplicity of hermeneutics of the same tradition." Panikkar, „The Hermeneutics of Hermeneutics...," [1963] *Philosophy Today* 2 (Fall 1967), p. 179.

[13] „One of the most characteristic phenomena of our age is undoubtedly the encounter of religions. It is happening today, perhaps for the first time, at the round table of world culture on an equal footing. The epochs of 'political Christianity,' of 'Empires,' of 'Colonialism,' are past

and we find ourselves better situated today to understand other religions from the interior. All that leads us to a qualified acceptance and elaboration of even theological 'pluralism,' or, in other words, of the basic possiblity of a multiplicity of hermeneutics of the same tradition." Panikkar, „The Hermeneutics of Hermeneutics…," [1963] *Philosophy Today* 2 (Fall 1967), p. 179.

[14]Panikkar, *Religionen….*, [1964] (1965), p. 150.

[15]Panikkar, *The Trinity…*, [1970] (1973), pp. 3-5.

[16]Panikkar, *Salvation in Christ:….*, (1972), p. 18.

[17] In the planetarian horizon people do not find the american flag planted in moon appropriatedly symbolised to represent the leap of humanity. So also others find God is not now in the planetarian horizon appropriate universal symbol. This is evident from the fact that „the three astronauts felt to speak the name of God when performing an action in the name of the whole human race." A humanist „will stress that his ultimate ideal--his God as as we could in point of fact say--is greater, broader and thus more valid than the, according to him, narrow conception of a personal God." Panikkar, *Worship…*, (1973), pp. 77-78.

[18] „Si une telle pensée peut poser pas mal de questions à notre topos, elle soulignera au moins la relativité de notre langage et poussera les chercheurs chrétiens, espérons-le, à ne pas se tourner seulement vers le passé chrétien institutionnel et traditionnel - sans le négliger toutefois- à dépasser un discours intra-culturel, pour s'ouvrir à la planète entière. Ce que le vingtième siècle finissant présente peut-e^tre comme caractéristique majeure, c'est cette diemsion planétaire des problèmes politiques, économiques, mais aussi intellectuels, culturels et religieux." R. Smet, Le Problème d'une théologie

<u>Hindoue-Chrétienne</u> selon Raymond Panikkar, (Louvain-La-Neuve: Centre d'Histoire des Religions, 1983), p. 6.

[19]Panikkar, „Metatheology...," *Concilium*, (June 1969), pp. 22-23.

[20] „Wenn Mensch und Kirche Pilger sind, ist es doch nicht erstaunlich, da$ die Theologie ebenfalls vorläufig ist, und da$ auch die Dogmen immerzu zum himmlischen Jerusalem unterwegs sind." Panikkar, *Kerygma und Indien:...,* (1967), p. 22.

[21]Panikkar, *Salvation in Christ:...,* (1972), p. 48.

[22]Panikkar, „Metatheology...," *Concilium*, (June 1969), p. 22.

[23] „Viele afrikanische Sprachen zum Beispiel kennen keine passenden Worte, um die Begriffe <u>Natur</u> und <u>Person</u> zu übersetzen, die dem Bewu$tsein der entsprechenden Völker völlig fremd sind. Diese Tatsache ist nicht nur ein Problem für die christliche Verkündigung, sondern sie könnte vielleicht für die Theologie von morgen zu einer Bereicherung und Verjüngung des zentralen Dogmas des Christentums führen." Panikkar, *Kerygma und Indien.....,* (1967), p. 22.

[24]Panikkar, „Metatheology...," *Concilium*, (June 1969), p. 26. „....the Christian *kerygma* should not first need to clear the ground by proving the existence of God and only then proceed further, but...it could find a meaningful *kerygma* by transmythicizing the God-talk." Panikkar, „Metatheology as Fundamental Theology," [1969] in *Myth, Faith and Hermeneutics:...,* (1979), p. 332.

[25]Panikkar, „ Metatheology...." *Concilium*, (June 1969), p. 25.

[26]Panikkar, „Metatheology...," *Concilium*, (June 1969), p. 24.

[27]Panikkar, „Metatheology...," *Concilium*, (June 1969), p. 26.

[28]Panikkar, „Metatheology...," *Concilium*, (June 1969), p. 26.

[29]Panikkar, „Metatheology...," *Concilium*, (June 1969), pp. 26-27. „Der Irrtum besteht darin, daß man versucht, das christliche Geheimnis mit dem Ausdruck gleichzusetzen, der in einem dieser besonderen Bezugssysteme vorliegt. Und diese Gleichsetzung ist fast unvermeidlich außerhalb des korrigierenden Moments eines theologischen oder selbst religiösen Pluralismus, im genauen Sinn dieses Wortes." Panikkar, *Kerygma und Indien....*, (1967), p. 22.

[30]Panikkar, *The Trinity...*, [1970] (1973), pp. 3-5.

[31]„R.Panikkar vient alors proposer une théologie hidou-chrétienne, c'est-à-dire non plus une adaptation de la pensée occidentale au <u>topos</u> de l'Inde, mais une pensée partant de l'hindouisme pour découvrir le Christ sans laisser celui-ci monopolisé par la seule pensée `méditerranéenne'." R. Smet, <u>Le Problème d'une théologie</u>..., (1983), p. 5.

[<u>32</u>] „Es ist die Mentalität der Mittelmeerländer, die sich zusammensetzt aus: jüdischen, hellenistischen, lateinischen, keltischen, gotischen und modernen Elementen....Der Irrtum besteht darin, da\$ man versucht, das christliche Geheimnis mit dem Ausdruck gleichzusetzen, der in einem dieser besonderen Bezugssysteme vorliegt. Und diese Gleichsetzung ist fast unvermeidlich au\$erhalb des korrigierenden Moments eines theologischen oder selbst religiösen Pluralismus, im genauen Sinn dieses Wortes." Panikkar, *Kerygma und*

Indien...., (1967), p. 22.

[33]„Elle est, dans une certaine mesure, nouvelle, prospectrice, prophétique[,] dirait-il, et elle rouvre une veine déjà exploitée dès l'époque patristique, par exemple par Justin et Clément d'Alexandrie." R. Smet. <u>Le Problème d'une théologie</u>..., (1983), pp. 5-6.

[34]Panikkar, *The Unknown....*, (1981), pp. 165-166. Panikkar *The Unknown....*, (1964), pp. 134-135. Panikkar, *Kerygma und Indien....*, (1967), p. 22.

[35]Panikkar, *The Unknown....*, (1981), pp. 165-166. Panikkar *The Unknown....*, (1964), pp. 134-135.

[36]„....that christianizing certain values (of Aristotelian philosophy in this case) does those values no harm, but rather clarifies them, makes them shine in a purer light. He considered that he was saying in his time what Aristotle would have wanted to say, not psychologically, perhaps, but ontologically, in so far as Aristotle tried to explain certain truths that are beyond words. ('Sub verbis latent significata verborum' is something that Saint Thomas never forgot. <u>Sum.Theol</u>. II-II, q. 8, a. 1.)" Panikkar, *The Unknown....*, (1981), p. 166. Panikkar *The Unknown....*, (1964), pp. 135-136.

[37]Panikkar, *Salvation in Christ:...*, (1972), p. 64.

[38] „Christian systematic theology has remained engulfed within Western culture and its intellectual history....To this day, Christian theology remains uninfluenced and unenriched by the majority of world religions. This is no longer possible....The encounter of world religions calls for the forging of a Christian systematic theology that will encompass within its horizons the religious experience of mankind....This is an unprecedented task. Never before in the history of Christianity has this challenge been raised." E. Cousins,

„....Theology of the future," *Cross Currents*, 29 (Summer 1979), pp. 145-146.

[39]E. Cousins, „....Theology of the future," *Cross Currents*, 29 (Summer 1979), p. 145.

[40]Panikkar, *The Trinity...*, [1970] (1973), p. 47.

[41]„Da gibt es nicht nur zwei, sondern wenigstens ein halbes Dutzend Kategorien, die, so scheint uns, imstande wären, daß Geheimnis der Trinität weitaus genauer oder doch wenigstens in neuen und ergänzenden Dimensionen darzustellen. Vielleicht wäre es aus der Perspektive indischen Denkens möglich, die griechisch-lateinische Spannung von Natur und Person zu überwinden....Kann man nicht annehmen, daß eine wirkliche Begegnung der Theologie, d.h. der Kirche, zum Beispiel mit Śaṅkara und Rāmānuja -- um die alte Parallele zu wahren -- von ebensolcher Bedeutung ist wie die „Entdeckung" Platons in den ersten Jahrhunderten der Kirche und die des Aristoteles im Mittelalter? Panikkar, *Kerygma und Indien....*, (1967), p. 22.

[42]Panikkar, *Salvation in Christ:....*, (1972), p. 72.

[43]Panikkar, *The Unknown.....*, (1981), p. 167. Panikkar *The Unknown.....*, (1964), p. 136.

[44]Panikkar, „The Jesus Debate" (Reviews of William Thompson's, <u>The Jesus Debate: A Survey and Synthesis</u> (Paulist Press, 1985)), <u>The Ecumenist</u> 24 (July-August, 1986) p. 73.

[45]R. Panikkar, *Salvation in Christ:....*, (1972), p. 73. Cf. Panikkar, „Metatheology...," *Concilium*, (June 1969), pp. 21-27.

[46]Panikkar, *Salvation in Christ:....*, (1972), p. 70.

[47]Panikkar, *Salvation in Christ:....*, (1972), p. 70 n.4.

[48]Panikkar, *Salvation in Christ:....*, (1972), p. 72.

[49]Panikkar, *The Unknown.....*, (1981), p. 167.

[50]Panikkar, *Salvation in Christ:...*, (1972), p. 81.

[51] „Doctrines are sometimes identical, personages (Jesus, Buddha, Krishna..) seem to [be so] similar that one cannot fail to see that 'our belief in the uniqueness of Christ is the greatest „stumbling block" for our brethren'." F. Gomes, „The Uniqueness and Universality of Christ," *East Asian Pastoral Review*, XX (No.1, 1983), p. 6.

[52] Panikkar, *The Unknown...*, (1981), p. 11.

[53] „Within Christianity we already find extreme attitudes that are falling into the very same mistakes, only in the opposite direction, that they are endeavouring to correct: if God was previously to the right, he is now to the far left. If Christ was a divine idol, now he is just a revolutionary Jew." Panikkar, *The Unknown....*, (1981), p. x. Cf. Panikkar, *Salvation in Christ:...*, (1972), p. 78.

[54] Panikkar, *The Unknown....*, (1981), pp. 7-8.

[55] Panikkar, *The Unknown...*, (1981), p. 165. Cf. Panikkar, *The Unknown...*, (1964), pp. 133-134.

[56] Panikkar, *The Unknown...*, (1964). Panikkar, *The Unknown...*, (1981).

[57] Panikakr, *Salvation in Christ...*, (1972).

[58]Panikkar, *The Trinity...*, [1970] (1973).

[59]E.H. Cousins, „....Theology of the future," *Cross Currents*, (Summer 1979), p. 148.

[60]Cf. H. Coward, „Panikkar's...Dialogue," *Cross Currents*, (Summer 1979), pp. 185-186. Cf. p. 183.

[61]According to Coward, all further *intra*-religious theologizing must take place within the context of (or at least with awareness of) *inter*-religious dialogue. Certainly this is exactly what Panikkar does in his book, *The Trinity and the Religious Experience of Man*. H. Coward, „Panikkar's...Dialogue," *Cross Currents*, (Summer 1979), p.

187.

BIBLIOGRAPHY

(The comprehensive bibliography has also been compiled with a view to the forthcoming books in the *Panikkar's Christological prayāṇa* series. The bibliography is divided into three parts: A. Primary Source: Panikkar's bibliography, has been divided into 1st books and 2nd articles [arranged chronologically]. B. Secondary source: the literature related to Panikkar, has been divided into 1. books/articles and 2. book reviews. C. Other sources: Books and articles consulted).)

A. Primary source: The Bibliography of Panikkar
1. Books
1948

__________. *F.H. Jacobi y la Filosofía del sentimiento*. Buenos Aires: Sapientia, 1948.

1949

__________. *Actas del Congreso Internacional de Filosofía*. Barcelona, 1948, Consejo Superior de Investigaciones Científicas, Madrid, 1949, 3 vols, ed., R. Panikkar.

1951

__________. *El Concepto de Naturaleza: Análisis Histórico y Metafísico de un Concepto*. Consejo Superior de Investigaciones Científicas, Madrid, 1951. Second Edition, Madrid: C.S.I.C., 1972.

1960

__________. *La India: Gente, Cultura, Creencias*. Madrid: Rialp, 1960.

--In Italian: *L'India: Popolazione cultura e credenze*. Morcellina: Brescia, 1964.

--In French: *Lettre sur l'Inde*. Tournai: Casterman, 1963.

1961

__________. *Patriotismo y Cristiandad*. Madrid: Rialp, 1961.

__________. *Ontonomía de la ciencia. Sobre el sentido de la Ciencia y sus relaciones con la Filosofía*. Madrid: Gredos, 1961.

1963

__________. *Humanismo y Cruz*. Madrid: Rialph, 1963.

__________. *L'incontro delle religioni del mondo contemporaneo: Morfosociologia dell'ecumenismo*. Roma: Edizioni Internazionali Sociali, 1963.

__________. *Die vielen Götter und der eine Herr: Beitrage zum Ökumenischen Gespräch der Weltreligionen*. Weilheim/Oberbayern: Otto Wilhelm Barth, 1963.

--In Spanish: *Los dioses y el Seen~or*. Buenos Aires: Columba, 1967.

1964

__________. *Religione e Religioni. Concordanze Funzionale ed Esistenziale delle Religioni. Studio Filosofico sulla natura storica e dinamica della religione*. Brescia: Morcelliana, 1964.

--In Spanish: *Religión y religiones*. Madrid: Gredos, 1965.

--In German: *Religionen und die Religion* München: Max Hüber, 1965.

__________. *The Unknown Christ of Hinduism*. London: Darton, Longman and Todd, 1964.

-English reprint, London: Darton, Longman & Todd 1968.

-English reprint, London: Darton, Longman & Todd 1977.

--(For the revised and enlarged edition see below under 1981.)

--In German: *Christus der Unbekannte im Hinduismus*. Luzern & Stuttgart: Räber, 1965.

--In Spanish: *El Cristo desconocido del Hinduismo*. Madrid: Marova & Barcelona: Fontanella, 1970.

--In French: *Le Christ et l'hindouisme: Une présence cachée*. Paris: Centurion, 1972.

--In Italian: *Il Cristo sconosciuto dell'Induismo*. Milano: Vitae Pensiero, 1975.

-Some parts also in *Māyā e Apocalisse. L'incontro del'Induismo e del Christianesimo*. Roma: Abete, 1966. pp. 133-164, 291-357.

__________. *Kultmysterium in Hinduismus und Christentum: Ein Beitrag zur vergleichenden Religionstheologie*. Freiburg & München: Karl Alber, 1964.

--In French: *Le Mystère du Culte dans l'Hindouisme et le Christianisme*. Paris: Cerf, 1970.

--Extract in German published as: "Aktion und Kontemplation im indischen Kultmysterium", *Una Sancta* (1966) p.145-150.

1966

__________. *Māyā e Apocalisse: L'incontro del'Induismo e del Christianesimo*. Roma: Abete, 1966.

--In Spanish: *Misterio y Revelación: Hinduismo y Cristianismo: Encuentro de dos Culturas*. Madrid: Marova, 1971.

--also in "Christus und Indien, Jesus und Wir", *Kairos* X (1968) pp. 115-132.

1967

__________. *Kerygma und Indien. Zur heilsgeschichtlichen Problematik der christlichen Begegnung mit Indien*. Hamburg: Herbert Reich, 1967.

__________. *Offenbarung und Verkundigung: Indische Briefe*. Freiburg: Herder, 1967.

__________. *Técnica y Tiempo. La Tecnocronía*. Buenos Aires: Columba, 1967.

1968

__________. *La Gioia Pasquale*. Vicenza: La Locusta, 1968.

1969

__________. *L'Homme qui devient Dieu. La foi dimension constitutive del'homme*. Paris: Aubier, 1969.

--In French "La Foi Dimension Constitutive de l'homme", *Archivio di Filosofia:Mito e Fede*, 34 (1966) pp. 17-44.

--Also as: "Faith as a Constitutive Human Dimension", in *Myth, Fith and Hermeneutics. Cross Cultural Studies*. New York: Paulist press, 1979, pp. 187-229.

1970

__________. *La presenza di Dio*. Vienza: La Locusta, 1970.

__________. *El Silencio del Dios. Un mensaje del Buddha al mundo actual: Contribución al estudio del ateísmo religioso*. Madrid: Guadiana, 1970.

--In Italian: *Il silenzio del Buddha*. Roma: Nuova Borla Editrice, 1984.

--Re-elaborated in Italian: *Il Silenzio di Dio: la Risposta del Buddha*. Roma, 1985.

--Also in English: "The Silence of the word: Non dualistic polarities." *Cross Currents* 24, 2-3 (Summer/Fall, 1974) pp. 154-171.

--Also as *The Silence of God: The Answer of the Buddha*. New York: Orbis Books, 1989.

__________. *The Trinity and World Religions. Icon-Person-Mystery*. Madras: The Christian Literature Society, 1970.

--*Revised and published as: The Trinity and the Religious Experience of Man: Icon-Person-Mystery*. London: Darton, Longman and Todd, 1973.

--Reprint: London: Darton, Longman and Todd; and New York: Orbis Books, 1975.

--Some parts in *Spiritualità indù: Lineamenti*. Brescia: Morcelliana, 1975.

--Also in *Kerygma und Indien. Zur heilsgeschichtlichen Problematik der christlichen begegnung mit Indien.* Hamburg: Herbert Reich, 1967. pp. 101-138.

--Also in "Towards an Ecumenical Theandric Spirituality", *Journal of Ecumenical Studies,* 5 (Summer 1968) 507-534.

1972

__________. *Dimensioni Mariane della Vita.* Vicenza: La Locusta, 1972.

--An extract published as: "The Marian Dimensions of Life", *Epiphany* 4 (Summar 1984) pp. 3-9.

__________. *Cometas: Fragmentos de un diario espiritual de la postguerra.* Madrid: Suramérica, 1972.

__________. *Salvation in Christ: Concreteness and Universality; The Supername.* Santa Barbara, 1972.

--Also in "The Meaning of Christ's name in the Universal Economy of Salvation," in *Documenta Missionalia 5: Evangelization Dialogue and Development,* (Selected papers of the International Theological Conference: `International Theological Congress on Evangelization' Nagpur India October, 1971. Dhavamony ed., (Roma 1972) pp. 195-218.

1973

__________. *Worship and Secular Man: An essay on the liturgical nature of Man, considering Secularization as a major phenomenon of our time and worship as an apparent fact of all times: A study towards an integral Anthropology.* London: Darton, Longman and Todd; and New York: Orbis Books, 1973.

--Reprint: London (DLT) and New York: Orbis Books 1975.

--In French: *Le culte et l'homme séculier.* Paris: Seuil, 1976.

--In Spanish: *Culto y secularización: Apuntes para una antropología liturgica.* Madrid: Marova, 1979.

1975

__________. *Spiritualità indù: Lineamenti.* Brescia: Morcelliana, 1975.

1977

__________. *The Vedic Experience. Mantraman~jari^: An Anthology of the Vedas for Modern Man and Contemporary Celebration.* London: Darton, Longman and Todd, (1977) reprint 1979.

--Revised Indian edition: Pondicherry: All India Books, 1983.

1978

__________. *The Intrareligious Dialogue.* New York: The Paulist Press, 1978.

-Indian edition: Bangalore: Asian Trading Corporation, 1984.

--In French: *Le dialogue intra-religieux.* Paris: Aubier, 1984.

--In Polish: Warszawa: Instytut Wyadawniczy PAX, 1985.

1979

__________. *Myth, Faith and Hermeneutics: Cross Cultural Studies.* New York: The Paulist Press, 1979.

-Indian edition: Bangalore: Asian Trading Corporation, 1983.

--In German: *Rückkehr zum Mythos* aus. Eng. Bettina Bäumer. Frankfurt: Isel Verlag, 1985.

- revised edition, US: Paulist Press 1999.

1981

__________. *The Unknown Christ of Hinduism: Towards an Ecumenical Christophany.* Revised and enlarged ed., London:

Darton, Longman & Todd; and New York: Orbis Books, 1981.

-Indian Edition: Bangalore: Asian Trading Corporation, 1982.

--In German: *Der unbekannte Christus im Hinduismus* Mainz: Matthias Grünewald, 1986.

--(For the first ed., see above under 1964).

1982

__________. *Blessed Simplicity: The Monk as Universal Archetype.* (In dialogue with E. Cousin, C. Tholens, M. Dardenne, A.Veilleux, M.B. Pennington & P. Soleri). New York: Seabury Press, 1982.

1993

__________ *The Cosmotheandric Experience: Emerging Religious Consciousness* edited by Scott Eastham. Maryknoll, N.Y. Orbis Books, 1993.

-------------- *A Dwelling Place for Wisdom.* Louisville, Kentucky Westminster John Knox Press, 1993

1995

-------------- *Invisible Harmony: Essays on Contemplation and Responsibility* edited by Harry James Cargas. Minneapolis: Augsburg Fortress Publishers,1995

__________ *Cultural Disarmament: The Way to Peace.* Louisville, Kentucky Westminster John Knox Press; 1995

2004

__________ Christophany: The Fullness Of Man. Mary Knoll: Orbis Books, , 2004.

2006

__________ The Experience of God: Icons of the Mystery (trans. by Joseph Cunneen). Fortress Press, 2006.

__________ Initiation to the Vedas. India: Motilal Banarsidass, , 2006

2009

__________ The Rhythm of Being. The Gifford Lectures. Mary Knoll Orbis Books, 2009,

2. Articles

1942

__________. "Investigación." *Revista de Filosofía*, no., 2 & 3, Consejo Superior de Investigaciones Cientificas, Madrid, 1942, pp. 389-398.

1944

__________. "Los productos químicos: su intervención en la curtición de las pieles." *Piel* 9/10, Madrid, 1944, pp. 72-75.

__________. "Visión de Síntesis del Universo." *Arbor: Revista General de la Investigación y la Cultura* 1 (Jan- Feb., 1944) pp. 5-40.

__________. "La Ciencia Biomatemática: Un Ejemplo de Síntesis Científica." *Arbor: Revista General de la Investigación y la Cultura* 1 (May-June 1944) pp. 349-372.

1945

__________. "El indeterminismo científico." *Anales de Física y Química* 41 (1945) p. 396.

__________. "El Sentido cristiano de la Vida. Su Aspecto Paradigmático en los primeros cristianos." *Arbor: Revista General de la Investigación y la Cultura* 4 (September - Octorber 1945) pp. 261-282.

-also in *Humanismo y Cruz* (Madrid 1963) 121-152.

1946

__________. "El sentido químico: de la industria de la piel." *Piel* - 29, Madrid (1946) pp. 11-16.

1947

__________. "Max Planck (1858-1947)." *Arbor: Revista General de la Investigación y la Cultura* 8 (Nov-Dece 1947) pp. 387-406.

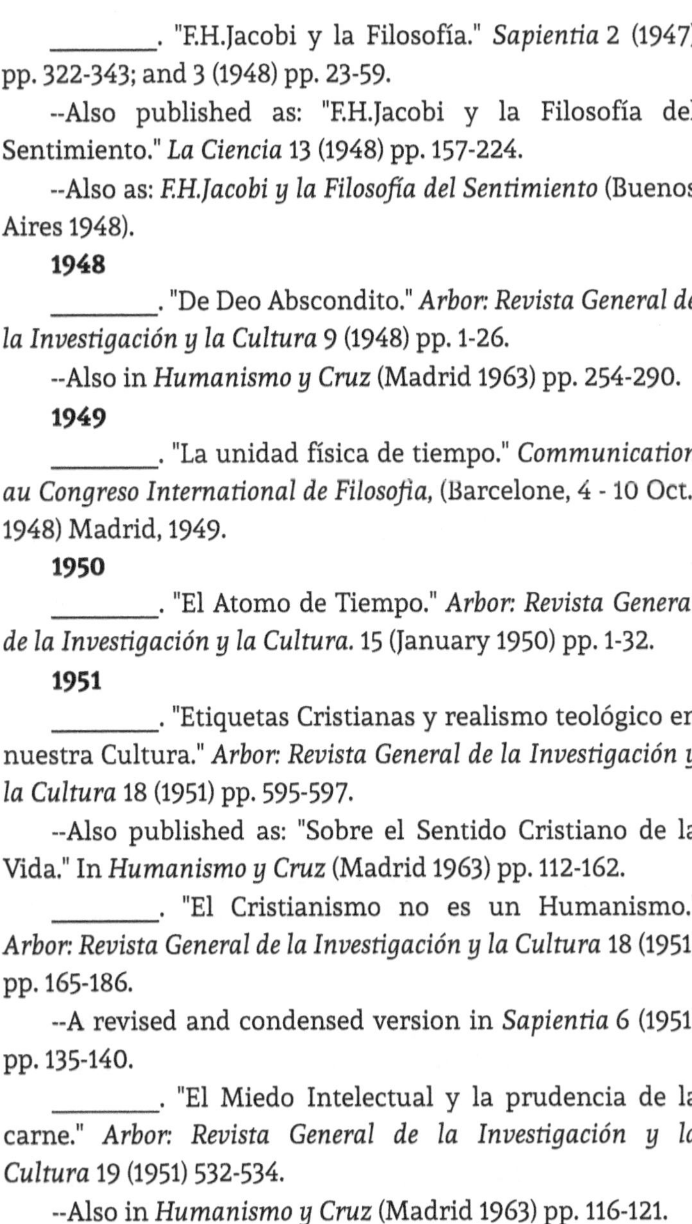

__________. "F.H.Jacobi y la Filosofía." *Sapientia* 2 (1947) pp. 322-343; and 3 (1948) pp. 23-59.

--Also published as: "F.H.Jacobi y la Filosofía del Sentimiento." *La Ciencia* 13 (1948) pp. 157-224.

--Also as: *F.H.Jacobi y la Filosofía del Sentimiento* (Buenos Aires 1948).

1948

__________. "De Deo Abscondito." *Arbor: Revista General de la Investigación y la Cultura* 9 (1948) pp. 1-26.

--Also in *Humanismo y Cruz* (Madrid 1963) pp. 254-290.

1949

__________. "La unidad física de tiempo." *Communication au Congreso International de Filosofia,* (Barcelone, 4 - 10 Oct., 1948) Madrid, 1949.

1950

__________. "El Atomo de Tiempo." *Arbor: Revista General de la Investigación y la Cultura.* 15 (January 1950) pp. 1-32.

1951

__________. "Etiquetas Cristianas y realismo teológico en nuestra Cultura." *Arbor: Revista General de la Investigación y la Cultura* 18 (1951) pp. 595-597.

--Also published as: "Sobre el Sentido Cristiano de la Vida." In *Humanismo y Cruz* (Madrid 1963) pp. 112-162.

__________. "El Cristianismo no es un Humanismo." *Arbor: Revista General de la Investigación y la Cultura* 18 (1951) pp. 165-186.

--A revised and condensed version in *Sapientia* 6 (1951) pp. 135-140.

__________. "El Miedo Intelectual y la prudencia de la carne." *Arbor: Revista General de la Investigación y la Cultura* 19 (1951) 532-534.

--Also in *Humanismo y Cruz* (Madrid 1963) pp. 116-121.

_________. "La Novedad que en el Concepto de Naturaleza introduce el Cristianismo." in *Tijdschrift voor Philosophie* 13 (June 1951) pp. 236-262.

_________. "Una cautela a los historiadores espan~oles." *Arbor: Revista General de la Investigación y la Cultura* 19 (1951) 532-534; and 20 (1951) pp. 112-113.

_________. "El Dinamismo de la Naturaleza." *Giornale di Metafisia* 6 (1951) 155-167.

_________. "La Naturaleza en la Ciencia Físico-Metemática." *Sapientia* 6 (1951) 36-46.

1952

_________. "Cristianidad y Cruz. Una Investigación Teológico-Histórica." *Arbor: Revista General de la Investigación y la Cultura* 19 (1951) 532-534; and 23 (1952) pp. 337-367.

--Also in *Humanismo y Cruz* (Madrid 1963) pp. 291-334.

_________. "La Eucaristía y la Resurreción de la Carne: Texto de la Comunicación al Congreso Eucarístico Internacional de Barcelona, May 1952." in *Humanismo y Cruz* (Madrid 1963) pp. 335-352.

_________. "Introduction." In Guitton Jean, *La Virgen Maria* (Madrid 1952) pp. 30-34.

_________. "Sind die Katholiken Katholisch? Das Corpus und seine Glieder." In *Wort und Wahrheit*, 7, Freiburg (1952) pp. 649-655.

1953

_________. "Le concept d'ontonomie." in Proceedings of the XIth. International Congress of Philosophy Bruxelles 20-26 August 1953, *Metaphysics and Ontology* Vol., III. Louvain: Nauwelaerts, 1953. pp. 182-188.

_________. "La Evolución del Patriotismo en Occidente." *Sapientia* 8 (1953) pp. 283-293.

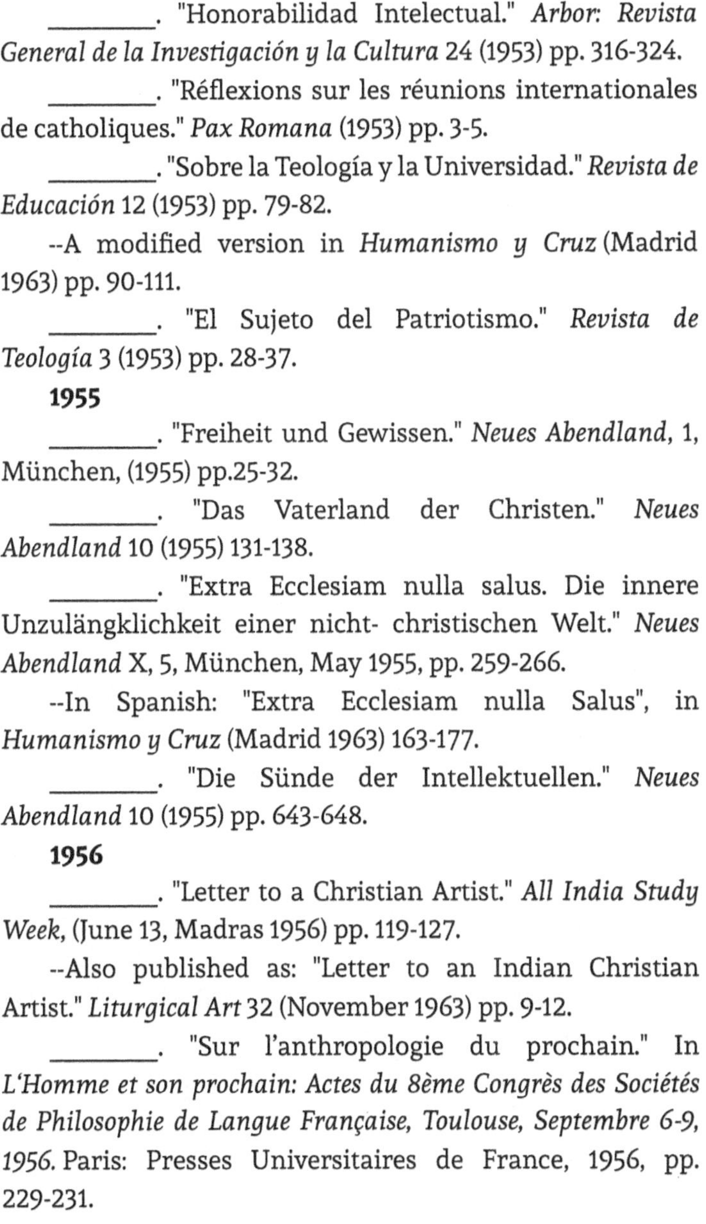

_________. "Honorabilidad Intelectual." *Arbor: Revista General de la Investigación y la Cultura* 24 (1953) pp. 316-324.

_________. "Réflexions sur les réunions internationales de catholiques." *Pax Romana* (1953) pp. 3-5.

_________. "Sobre la Teología y la Universidad." *Revista de Educación* 12 (1953) pp. 79-82.

--A modified version in *Humanismo y Cruz* (Madrid 1963) pp. 90-111.

_________. "El Sujeto del Patriotismo." *Revista de Teología* 3 (1953) pp. 28-37.

1955

_________. "Freiheit und Gewissen." *Neues Abendland*, 1, München, (1955) pp.25-32.

_________. "Das Vaterland der Christen." *Neues Abendland* 10 (1955) 131-138.

_________. "Extra Ecclesiam nulla salus. Die innere Unzulängklichkeit einer nicht- christischen Welt." *Neues Abendland* X, 5, München, May 1955, pp. 259-266.

--In Spanish: "Extra Ecclesiam nulla Salus", in *Humanismo y Cruz* (Madrid 1963) 163-177.

_________. "Die Sünde der Intellektuellen." *Neues Abendland* 10 (1955) pp. 643-648.

1956

_________. "Letter to a Christian Artist." *All India Study Week*, (June 13, Madras 1956) pp. 119-127.

--Also published as: "Letter to an Indian Christian Artist." *Liturgical Art* 32 (November 1963) pp. 9-12.

_________. "Sur l'anthropologie du prochain." In *L'Homme et son prochain: Actes du 8ème Congrès des Sociétés de Philosophie de Langue Française, Toulouse, Septembre 6-9, 1956.* Paris: Presses Universitaires de France, 1956, pp. 229-231.

________. "Christian Meaning and Human Values." *The King's Rally* 33 (1956) pp. 25-32.

________."Die Existentielle Phänomenologie der Wahrheit." in *Philosophisches Jahrbuch der Görres Gesellschaft* 64 (1956) pp. 27-54.

--"The Existential Phenomenology of Truth." *Philosophy Today* 2 (Spring 1958) pp. 13-21.

--In Italian: "La fenomenologia esistenziale della veritá," in *Māyā e Apocalisse. L'incontro del'Induismo e del Christianesimo.* Roma: Abete, 1966, pp. 241-289.

________. "If God exists." *Vedanta Kesari* (December 1956).

--in *The Unknown Christ of Hinduism.* London: Darton, Longman and Todd, 1964. pp. 70-73.

--in *The Unknown Christ of Hinduism: Towards an Ecumenical Christophany.* London: Darton, Longman & Todd; and New York: Orbis Books, 1981. pp. 102-105.

1957

________. "Does Indian Philosophy need Re-orientation? The recovery of its theological background for the reorientation of Indian Philosophy." *Philosophy East and West* (April 1957) pp. 23-28.

--In Italian: "L'Esigenza di un Nuovo Orientamento della Filosofia indiana." in *Māyā e Apocalisse. L'Incontro dell'Induismo e del Cristianesimo.* Roma: Abete, 1966, pp. 33-69.

________. "Mission of the Laity in the Church." *The King's Rally* (Madras) 34 (1957) pp. 123-129.

________. "The Sanctity of St. John of the Cross and of St. Theresa." in *Prabuddha Bharata*, III (1957) pp. 1-6.

--Also published as: "Some aspects of Spirituality of St. John of the Cross and of St. Theresa." *The Living Word* 76

(November - December 1970) pp. 258-268.

__________. "Some Phenomenological Aspects of Hindu Philosophy Today." *Oriental Thought* 3 (1957) pp. 151-191.

--Also published as: "Contemporary Hindu Spirituality." *Philosophy Today* 3 (Summer 1959) pp. 112-127.

-- In German, "Aspekte heutiger Hindu-Spiritualität." (trans, by Heiler A.M.), in Heiler A.M. ed., *Inter Confessiones: Beiträge zur FÖrderung des Interkonfessionellen und Interreligiösen Gesprächs Friedrich Heiler zum Gedächtnis aus Anlass seines 80 Geburtstage am 30.1.1972* (Marburg 1972) pp. 132-153.

1958

__________. "The Theological Basis for Christian-non-Christian co-operation in Social Thought and Action," *Religion and Society* 5 (March 1958) 29-36.

--In Italian: "Basi Teologiche per una cooperazione attiva fra Cristiani e non Cristiani." in *Māyā e Apocalisse: L'Incontro dell'Induismo e del Cristianesimo.* Roma: Abete, 1966, pp. 175-184.

__________. "The Integration of Indian Philosophical and Religious Thought." *Religion and Society* 5 (June 1958) 23-29.

--A modified version: "Indian Philosophy and Christian Doctrine." *Frontier* (October 1958) pp. 271-274.

--In Spanish: "La integración del pensamiento filosófico y religioso de la India." *Orbis catholicus,* 7 (Barcelona 1960) pp. 1-7.

-Also in *Criterio* 36 (Buenos Aires, 1963) pp. 247-248.

--In French: "Integration de la Pensée philosophique et religieuse de l'Inde." *Bulletin du Cercle Saint Jean-Baptiste* 20 (February 1963) pp. 16-22.

--In Italian: "Il Problema della integrazione del Pensiero filosofico e religioso indiano nella teologia." in *Māyā e*

Apocalisse: L'incontro dell'Induismo e del Cristianesimo. Roma: Abete, 1966 pp. 165-173.

1959

__________. "Ishwara and Christ as a Philosophical Problem." *Religion and Society* 6 (1959) pp. 8-16.

--Also published as "The Is'vara of Vedānta and the Christ of

the Trinity as Philosophical Problem." in *Atti del XII Congresso Internatizonale di Filosofie (Venezia 12-18 Settembre 1958) Vol., X: no., 50: Filosofie Orientali e Pensiero Occidentale* (Firenze 1960) pp. 153-160.

--In German: "Der Ishwara des Vedanta und der Christus der Trinität. Eine Philosophisches Problem." *Antaios* 2 (1961) pp. 446-455.

--Also in *The Unknown Christ of Hinduism.* London: Darton, Longman and Todd, 1964. pp. 126-131.

--Also in *The Unknown Christ of Hinduism: Towards an Ecumenical Christophany.* London: Darton, Longman & Todd, and New York: Orbis Books, 1981, pp. 155-162.

__________. "Eine Betrachtung über Melchisedech." *Kairos* 1 (1959) pp. 5-17.

--Also in *Melchisedech: Urgestalt der ökumene.* Freiburg: Herder 1979.

--In Italian: "Meditazioni su Melchisedech." in *Māyā e Apocalisse. L'Incontro dell'Induismo e del Cristianesimo.* Roma: Abete, 1966, pp. 185-203.

--"Christ Abel and Melchizedek: The Church and the nonAbrahamic religions." *Jeevadhara*, V (Sep-Oct., 1971) pp. 391-403.

__________. CUTTAT J.A. *Vergeistingungs'Technik' und Umgestalltung in Christus,* (Comment), *Kairos* 1 (1959) pp. 18-30; 2 (1960) pp. 44-45.

_________. `The Symbol He is'. Contribution to *Swami Parama Arubi Anandam* (Fr Monchanin. A memorial), Tiruchirappalli: Saccidanda Ashram, 1959, pp. 127-131.

1960

_________. "Keine christlicher Yoga, aber Yoga ist eine nochoffene christliche Propädeutik." *Kairos* 2 (1960) pp. 44-45.

_________. "Um das Religiöse Gespräch." *Kairos* 2 (1960) p. 180.

_________. "Konferenzen der `Pax Romana' in Manila 26.12.1959 bis 8.1.1960." *Kairos* 2 (1960) pp. 106-107.

_________. "The Brahman of the Upaniṣads and the God of the Philosophers." *Religion and Society* 17 (Sept., 1960) no., 2. pp. 12-19.

--In German: "Das Brahman der Upaniṣaden und der Gott der Philosophen." *Kairos* 3 (1961) 1/2 pp. 182-188.

1961

_________. HACKER P., *Magie, Gott Persona und Gnade im Hinduismus* (Comment) in *Kairos* 2 (1960) pp. 225-233; 3 (1961) pp. 112-114.

_________. "La Demitolgizzazione nell'incontro del Cristianesimo e l'Induismo." *Archivo di Filosofia: Il Problema della Demitizzazione.* (Padua: Cedam, 1961) pp. 243-266.

--In Spanish: "El Encuentro con la India", in *Los Dioses y el Sen~or* (Buenos Aires 1967) pp. 45-67.

_________. "Nota al Padre Dhanis", *Achivio di Fisosofía* 19 (1961) pp. 333-334.

_________. "La espiritualidad hindú", *Nuestro Tiempo* 8 (October 1961) pp. 1181-1207.

_________. "Eucharistischer Glaube und Idolatrie." *Kairos* 3 (1961) pp. 85-90.

_________. "Hinduismus und Magie", *Kairos* 3 (1961) pp. 112-114.

_________. "Pluralismus, Toleranz und Christenheit." in *Pluralismus, Toleranz und Christenheit*, Hans Schomerus (u.a); Nürnberg: Abendländische Akademie, 1961, pp. 117-142.

--Also in "Tolerance, ideology and Myth." Panikkar, *Myth, Faith and Hermeneutics*. New York: The Paulist Press, 1979, pp. 20-33.

--In Spanish: in *Los Dioses y el Sen~or* (Buenos Aires 1967) pp. 116-146.

_________. "La Tempiternidad. La Misa como `Consecratio Temporis'." In *Sanctum Sacrificum: Proceedings of the 'V Congreso Eucarístico Nacional'.* Zaragoza (1961) pp. 75-93.

_________."Hinduism and Christianity." in *Student World*, LV, 3 (Genève, 1963) pp. 304-323.

--Also in *Cross Currents*, XIII (1963) pp. 87-101.

--In French: "Hindouisme et christianisme." *Mitte me* 5 (1963) pp. 1-9.

1962

_________. "Le Fondement du Pluralisme Herméneutique dans l'hindouisme." *Demitizzazione e Immagine.* Padua: Cedam, 1962, pp. 243-259.

--In Spanish: *Los Dioses y el Sen~or*. Buenos Aires 1967, pp. 67-97.

--In German: "Die Begründung des hermeneutischen Pluralismus in Hinduismus." *Kerygma und Mythos: Entmythologisierung und Bild.* VI, Band II, Hamburg: Herbert Reich, 1964.

_________. "Letter to a Christian Student of Hinduism." *Logos* (Colombo) 3 (October 1962) pp. 1-5.

________. "Forme e crisi della spiritualità contemporanea." *Studi Cattolici*, no., 33, (Roma, June, 1962) pp. 9-23.

________. "Spätantiker Heidentum (Comments)." by Raimundo Panikkar and E. von Ivanka in *Kairos* 4 (1962) pp. 83-90; 5 (1963) pp. 69-70.

________. "Zur Einführung in die indische Weltanschauung." In *Stimmen der Zeit* 170. Bd. 87. (Freiburg 1962) pp. 177-185.

--in English: "Indian Philosophy, an Introduction", *Philosophy Today* 8 (Summer 1964) pp. 110-117.

1963

________. "Sur l'herméneutique de la Tradition dans l'hindouisme. Pour un Dialogue avec le Christianisme." in *Archivio di Filosofia: Ermeneutica e Tradizione* 31 (Paris: Vrin; and Roma: Istituto die studi filosofici, 1963) pp. 342- 364.

--In Italian: "Sull'ermeneutica della Tradizione nell'Induismo. Per un dialogo con il Christianesimo", *Humanitas* 19 (1964) pp. 953-983.

--"The Hermeneutics of Hermeneutics. Reflections on the hermeneutics of Tradition in Hinduism in view of a dialogue with Christian thought." *Philosophy Today* 2 (Fall 1967) pp. 166-183.

--In German: "Über die Hermeneutik der Tradition im Hinduismus", in *Kerygma und Indian: Zur heilsgeschichlichen Problematik der christlichen Begegnung mit Indien* (Hamburg 1967) pp. 67-90.

________. "La Metafísica de los textos hindués sobre la creación." *Atlántida* 1 (Jan. - Feb. 1963) pp. 86-90.

________. "Progresso Scientifico e Contesto Culturale: Discussion." Raimundo Panikkar and others, *Civiltá delle Macchine* (May - June 1963) pp. 19-29.

__________. "Panikkar Raimundo, "Una Meditazione teologica sulle tecniche di Comunicazione", *Studi Cattolici* 7 (1963) pp. 11-16.

--In Spanish: "Una consideración teológica sobre los medios de comunicación social." *Atlántida* 1/4 (Jul.-Aug. 1963) pp. 435-441.

__________. "El espíritu religioso del pueblo castellano." *Nuestro Tiempo* (Sep. 1963) pp. 3-16.

__________. "Sugerencias para una Teofísica." *Convivium* 21 (1966) pp. 235-243.

--in Italian: "Introduzione alla Teosofica." *Civiltá delle Macchine*, Roma (Nov. 5, 1963) pp. 28-32.

__________. "Communication sur l'Inde face à l'athéisme de l'Occident." in Veuillot P., Henry A. M., and others, eds., *L'Athéisme, Tentation du Monde, Réveil des chrétiens?* Paris: Cerf, 1963, pp. 53-57.

__________. "La Confidencia. Análisis de un sentimiento." in *Rivista Espan~ola de Filosofía*. Madrid: Consejo Superior de Investigaciones Cientifícas, 1963, pp.43-62.

__________. "Der Zerbrochene Krug, zur indischen Symbolhaftigkeit," *Antaios* 4 (1963) pp. 556-571.

--Also in *Kultmysterium in Hinduismus und Christentum. Ein Beitrag zur vergleichenden Religionstheologie.* Freiburg & München: Karl Alber, 1964, pp. 135-146.

__________. "Europa und die Frage nach der kulturellen Einheit der Menschheit," in *Das Europänische Erbe in der Heutigen Welt.* Edited by Walter Werr. Nürnberg: Abendländishe Akademie E.V., 1963.

1964

__________. "Technique et Temps: la Technochronie", *Archivio di Filosofia: Tenica e Casistica.* 32 (1964) pp. 195-229.

--An extract: "Technology and Time, Technochrony", *Pax Romana Journal* (February 1967) pp. 3-6.

__________. "Das erste Bild des Buddha. Zur Einführung in den buddhistischen Apophastismus", *Antaios* 6 (1964) pp. 373-385.

--In Italian: "La Prima Immagine del Buddha. Per una introduzione all'apofatismo buddhista", *Humanits* 21 (June 1966) pp. 608-622.

--In German: "Das erste Bild des Buddha", in *Kerygma und Indian: Zur heilsgeschichlichen Problematik der christlichen Begegnung mit Indien.* Hamburg: Herbert Reich, 1967, pp. 91-100.

1965

__________. "Morale du Mythe et Mythe de la Morale: Mythologie et Logomythologie." *Archivio di Filsosofia: Demitizzazione e Morale* 33 (Aubier-Montaigne, 1965) pp. 393-413.

--"Morality and Myth. The Moral of Myth and the Myth of Morals." In *Myth, Fith and Hermeneutics: Cross Cultural Studies.* New York, Ramsey, Toronto 1979, pp. 37-64.

__________. "Advaita and Bhakti, Lettera da Vrindaban", *Humanits* 20 (1965) pp. 991-1001.

--In German: "Die Begegnung indischer Weisheit mit christlicher Liebe", in *Kerygma und Indian: Zur heilsgeschichlichen Problematik der christlichen Begegnung mit Indien.* Hamburg: Herbert Reich, 1967, pp. 59-65.

--"Advaita and Bhakti. A Letter from Vrindaban." in *Bhagawan Das Commemoration Volume* (Varanasi 1969).

--Also "Advaita e Bhakti, love and identity in a Hindu Christian Dialogue." *Journal of Ecumenical Studies* 7 (Spring 1970) pp. 299-309.

--Also in *Myth, Faith and Hermeneutics*. New York: The Paulist Press, 1979, pp. 277-289.

--Also in *Revista de Occidente*, no., 91 (1970) pp. 38-52.

__________. "Letter from Holy Mount Athos." *Sobornost*, IV, no., 12, (1965) pp. 726-731.

--In French: "Lettre du Saint mont Athos." *Christus* 12 (July 1965) pp. 418-424.

__________. "Relation of Christians to their non-Christian Surroundings." *Indian Ecclesiastical Studies* 4 (July - August 1965) pp. 303 - 348.

--Also in Joseph Neuner, ed., *Christian Revelation and World Religions*. London: Burns and Oates, 1967, pp. 143-184.

--Also published as: "Christians and so-called 'non-Christians'." *Cross Currents* 22 (Summer-Fall 1972) pp. 282-308.

--Also in D.J. Elwood, ed., *What Asian Christians are Thinking. A Theological Source Book*. Quezon City, 1976, pp. 339-376.

--In German "Das Verhältnis der Christen zu ihrer nicht-christlichen Welt." in *Kerygma und Indian: Zur heilsgeschichlichen Problematik der christlichen Begegnung mit Indien*. Hamburg, 1967, pp. 29-58.

1966

__________. "L'Eglise et les Religions du Monde." *Orient* 8 (1966) pp. 7-15.

--Italian: "La Chiesa e le religioni del mondo." (trans by M. Riccati Di Ceva), *Humanitas*, (Brescia, Feb.-March, 1966) pp. 168-173.

--"Church and the World Religions." *Religion and Society*, XIV, Nr. 2 (Bangalore, 1967) pp. 59-63.

__________. "Hinduism / Christianity", (Excerpt from *The Unknown Christ of Hinduism*. London: Darton, Longman and

Todd, 1964). *Jubilee* 13, (Jan. 1966) pp. 28-33.

________. "La Foi Dimension Constitutive de l'homme", *Archivio di Filosofia:Mito e Fede,* 34 (1966) pp. 17-44.

--Also published as: *L'Homme qui devient Dieu: La foi dimension constitutive de l'homme.* Paris, 1969.

--"Faith - A Constitutive Dimension of Man", *Journal of Ecumenical Studies* 8, no., 2 (Spring 1971) pp. 223-254.

--Also as: "Faith as a Constitutive Human Dimension", in *Myth, Faith and Hermeneutics. Cross Cultural Studies.* New York: Paulist press, 1979, pp. 187-229.

________. "The Crisis of Madhyamika and Indian Philosophy Today." *Philosophy East and West* 16 (1966) pp. 117-131.

--In Italian: "La Crisi della Filosofia Indiana." in *Māyā e Apocalisse: 'Incontro dell'Induismo e del Cristianesimo.* Roma: Abete, 1966, pp. 99-130.

________. "Philosophen-Kongress in Indien", *Kairos* 8 (1966) p. 67.

________. "Philosophy and Theology: Reason and Faith - An Essay in Terminological Clarification." in *The Concept of Philosophy* (Banaras s. d.) pp. 507-534.

--In Italian: "L'Esigenza di un nuovo orientamento della Filosofia indiana." in *Māyā e Apocalisse L'Incontro dell'Induismo e del Cristianesimo.* Roma: Abete, 1966, pp. 33-69.

________. "La Problematica dell'aggiornamento Monastico." in *Visioni Attuali sulla Vita Monastica.* Montserrat, 1966, pp. 221-230.

--"The Problem of Monastic Aggiornamento", *The Monastic Studies* (1969) pp. 103-112.

________. "Aktion und Kontemplation im indischen Kultmysterium", *Una Sancta* (1966) pp. 145-150. [Extract of the book: *Kultmysterium in Hinduismus und Christentum. Ein Beitrag zur vergleichenden Religionstheologie.* Freiburg & München: Karl Alber, 1964.]

1967

__________. "La faute originante, ou l'immolation créatrice: le mythe de Prajapati." *Archivio di Filosofia: Il Mito della Pena,* 35 (1967) pp. 65- 100.

--Also as "La faute originante." *Le mythe de la peine.* Aubier- Montaigne, Paris, 1967.

--"The Myth of Prajapti. The originating Fault or Creative Immolation", in *Myth, Faith and Hermeneutics.* New York: The Paulist Press, 1979, pp. 65-95.

__________. "Intervention." in A. Caracciolo, "Le Mal dans l'experience religieuse." *Archivio di Filosofia: Il Mito della Pena,* 35 (1967) pp. 265-281.

__________. "Intervention." in S. Lyonnet, "La Problématique du Péché originel dans le Nouveau Testament." *Archivio di Filosofia: Il Mito della Pena,* 35 (1967) pp. 101-120.

__________. "The European University Tradition and the Renascent World Cultures: A Challenge to the European University." *Geneva, World councils of Churches: Christian presence in higher Education.* Basal, 1967, pp. 72-87.

--Also in *Communio Viatorum* (January - February 1968) pp. 1-15.

__________. "Dialogue between Ian and Ray: Is Jesus Christ unique?" Raimuno Panikkar and Ian Stephens, *Theoria to Theory,* I (Jan., 1967) pp. 127-137.

1968

__________. "Herméneutique de la liberté de la religion. La Religion comme liberté." *Achivio di Fisosofia: L'ermeneutica della Liberté Religiosa,* edited by Castelli 36

(Paris: Aubier-Montaigne, 1968) pp. 57-86.

--"Hermeneutics of Religious Freedom: Religion as Freedom." in *Myth, Faith and Hermeneutics*. New York: The Paulist Press, 1979, pp. 419- 460.

--In German: "Hermeneutik der religiösen Freiheit: Die Religion als Freiheit, in *Kerygma und Mythos*, VI, Band V, Hamburg: Herbert Reich, 1974, pp. 118-136.

__________. "Intervention", in RICOEUR P. "Approche Philosophique du Concept de Liberté religieuse." *Achivio di Fisosofia: L'ermeneutica della Liberté Religiosa*, edited by Castelli 36 (Paris: Aubier-Montaigne, 1968) pp. 253-252.

__________. "The God of Being and the `Being' of God: An Exploration", *Harvard Divinity Bulletin* (Spring 1968) pp. 12-16.

--A modified version: "God of Silence." *Indian Journal of Theology* XXI (Jan-Jun., 1972) pp. 116-124.

--Also as: "The God of being and the `Being' of God. Religion and Atheism", in *Myth, Faith and Hermeneutics*. New York: The Paulist Press, 1979, pp. 349-360.

--Also in *El Silencio del Dios. Un mensaje del Buddha al mundo actual: Contribución al estudio del ateísmo religioso*. Madrid: Guadiana, 1970.

__________."The Internal Dialogue--The Insufficiency of the so-called phenomenological `Epoché' in the Religious Encounter," *Religion and Society* XV, 3. (1968) pp. 55-66.

--Also in *The Intra-Religious Dialogue*. New York: Ramsey, 1978, pp. 39-52.

__________. "Ogni autentica Religione e via di salvezza." In *Incontro tra le religioni, Doucmenti Nuovi*. Roma: Mondadori (1968) pp. 107-123.

__________. "Religionwissenschaft oder Religionsgeschihte?" *Kairos* 10 (1968) pp. 56-57.

________. "Towards an Ecumenical Theandric Spirituality." *Journal of* Ecumenical *Studies* 5 (Summer 1968) pp. 507- 534.

--In German: "Idolatrie, Personalismus, Advaita", in *Kerygma und Indian: Zur heilsgeschichlichen Problematik der christlichen Begegnung mit Indien.* Hamburg, 1967, pp. 101-138.

--also in *The Trinity and World Religions: Icon. Person. Mystery.* Madras: The Christian Literature Society, 1970.

________. "Christus und Indien, Jesus und Wir." [Ein Gespräch in Rom über *Māyā e Apocalisse. L'incontro del'Induismo e del Christianesimo*, von Raimundo Panikkar, Roma: Abete, 1966.] X *Kairos* (1968) pp. 115-132.

1969

________. "Le Silence et la Parole. Le Sourire du Bouddha." Achivio *di Fisosofia L'Analisi del Linguaggio Teologico Il Nome di Dio* 37 (1969) pp. 121-134.

--In Spanish: "La Sonrisa de Buda", *La Revista de Occidente* 76 (July 1969).

--Revised version in English: "Nirvāna and the Awareness of the Absolute." in J.P. Whelan, ed., *The God Experience: Essays in Hope: The Cardinal Bea Lectures, Vol., II.* New York, Toronto: Newmann Press, 1971, pp. 81-99.

--Again: "Nirvāna and The Awareness of the Absolute." *Dialogue* 9 (Colombo 1982) pp. 104-120.

--Again as: "Silence and the Word. The Smile of the Buddha", in *Myth, Faith and Hermeneutics.* New York: The Paulist Press 1979 pp. 257-276.

________. "Confrontation between Hinduism and Christ", *New Blackfriars* 50 (January 1969) pp. 197-204.

--Also in *Logos* (Colombo) 10 (1969) pp. 43-51.

________. "The Alternative. A Kairological Meditation on the All India Seminar on the Church in India." *The Examiner* (Bombay, April 12, 1969) pp. 229-230 and continued in *The Examiner* (Bombay, April 19, 1969) pp. 245-246.

--In Italian: "L'Alternativa. Meditazione Kairologica sulla conferenza panindiana e sulla Chiesa in India." *Humanitas* 24 (December 1969) pp. 1141-1153.

________. "Metatheology or Diacritical Theology as Fundamental Theology". In *Concilium* (Nijmegen) VI, no., 5 (June 1969) pp. 21-27.

--Also in *Myth, Faith and Hermeneutics*. New York: The Paulist Press, 1979, pp. 321-334.

________. "An open letter to Mr. Shusaku Endo on his book `The Silence'." *The Japan Missionary Bulletin* XXIII (November 1969) pp. 623-624.

________. "La Présence de Dieu." *La Vie Spirituelle* (December 1969) pp. 527-533.

________. "Christianity and the World Religions." In *Christianity* [Collective work]. Patiala: Punjabi University (1969) pp. 78-127.

________. "The People of God and the Cities of Man." Setphen Verney, ed., *The People and Cities*. London: Collins, Fontana Books, 1969, pp. 190-219.

________. "Zero." *Frontier* 12 (1969) pp. 252-254.

--In German: "Die Null: Ungestalt des Nichts." in J. Tenzler, ed., *Urbild und Abglanz. Beiträge zu einer Synopse von Weltgestalt und Glaubenswirklichkeit* (Regensburg 1972) pp. 175-178.

________. "Algunos aspectos de la espiritualidad hindú," in, L. Sala Balust and Jiménez Duque (eds) *Historia de espiritualidad*. Barcelona: Flors, 1969, pp. 433-542.

--In Italian: *Spiritualità indù: Lineamenti.* Brescia: Morcelliana, 1975.

1970

_________. "Le Sujet de l'Infaillibilité. Solipsisme et Vérification." *Archivio di Filosofia: L'Infallibilità, L'aspetto Filosofico e Teologico.* 38 (1970) pp. 423-445.

--In Spanish: "El Sujeto de la infalibilidad." *Revista de Occidente* 108 (March 1972).

--"The Subject of Infallibility. Solipsism and Verification" in *Myth, Faith and Hermeneutics.* New York: The Paulist Press, 1979, pp. 389-417.

--In German: "Das Subjekt der Unfehlbarkeit. Solipsismus und Verifikation" in *Kerygma und Mythos VI: Aspect der unfehlbarkeit Kritische Untersuchungen und Interpretationen* edited by Dr. Franz Theunis, Lüwen/ Belgien, Hamburg: Herbert Reich, 1975, pp.178-193.

_________. "Je crois." *Parole et Mission.* Paris, Cerf, 50 (May-1970) pp. 258-260.

_________. "Machines and Men." *Frontier* 13 (June 1970) pp. 258-260.

_________. "Indirect Methods in the Missionary Apostolate: Some Theological Reflections." In *Indian Journal of Theology* 19 (Jul-Dec., 1970) pp. 111-113.

_________. "Buddhismo è Ateismo?" in *L'Ateismo Contemporaneo*, Vol., IV: *Il Cristianesimo di fronte all'Ateismo* (Torino 1970) pp. 449-476.

_________. "Cristianismo y Culturas." *Diccionario Salvat.* Barcelona, 1970, pp. 12-13.

_________. "Fe y Creencia. Sobre la Experiencia multireligiosa." in *Homenaje a Xavier Zubiri* Vol., 2. (Madrid: E'ditorial Moneda y Crédito, 1970) pp. 435-459.

--A shortened and revised version in English: "Faith and Belief: A Multireligious Experience. An Objectified Autobiographical Fragment." *Anglican Theological Review*. III, no., 4 (October, 1971) pp.219-237.

--Also in *The Intra-Religious Dialogue*. New York, 1978, pp. 1-23.

__________."Menneskehedens enhed menneskehedens Splittelse." *Nordisk Missions-Tidsskrift* I, no., 81. Copenhaguen (1970) pp. 92-98.

__________. "Secularization and Worship." in Von Bussum, ed., *Worship and Secularization* (Amsterdam 1970) pp. 28-71.

--Also in *Studia Liturgica* 7 (1970) pp. 28-71.

__________. "The Ultimate Experience: The Ways of East and West." in G. Devine, ed., *New Dimensions in Religious Experience: Proceedings of the XVI Annual Convention of the College Theology Society*. New York: Alba House, Staten Island, 1970, pp. 69-93.

--A revised version in *Indian Ecclesiastical Studies* 10, no., 1, (January, 1971) pp. 18-39.

--Also published as: "The Supreme Experience: The Ways of East and West," in *Myth, Fith and Hermeneutics: Cross Cultural Studies.* New York: The Paulist Press, pp. 291-317.

__________. "Die Zukunft kommt nicht später." in L. Reinisch, ed., *Vom Sinn der Tradition*. München: C.H. Beck, 1970, pp. 53-64.

__________. "The Myth of Incest as Symbol for Redemption in Vedic India." In *Types of Redemption: Contributions to the Thema of the Study Conference held at Jerusalem--14th to 19th July, 1968*. ed. by R.J. Zwi Werblosky and C. Jouco Bleeker. London: E.J.Brill, 1970, pp. 130-143.

________. "La Alternativa: Meditación Kairológica sobre un seminario panindio que estudie la situación de la Iglesia en la India." In *Convivium*, no., 32 (1970) pp. 3-14.

1971

________. "Die Philosophie in der geistigen Situation der Zeit." in *Akten des XIV. Internationalen Kongress für Philosophie, Wien 2-9 Sept. 1968.* Vienna: Herder, 1971, pp. 75-87.

--also as "The Philosophical Tradition." in *Myth, Faith and Hermeneutics.* New York: The Paulist Press, 1979, pp. 335-348.

________. "La loi du Karma et la dimension historique de l'Homme." *Archivo di Filosofia: Ermeneutica e Escatologia,* 39 (1971) pp. 205-230.

--"The Law of karman and the historical dimension of man", *Philosophy East and West* 22 (1972) pp. 25-43.

--Also in *Myth, Fith and Hermeneutics. Cross Cultural Studies.* New York: The Paulist Press, 1979. pp. 361-388.

________. "Il messagio dell'India di ieri al mondo di oggi" *Filosofia,* no., I (January, 1971) pp. 3-28.

--"The Message of Yesterday's India to Today's World." *Religion and Society* 27 (1981) pp. 64-74.

________. "Indology as a Cross-Cultural Catalyst. A New Task of Indological Studies: Cross-Cultural Fertilization." *Numen,* 18 (Dec. 1971) pp. 173-179.

________. "Die Fata Morgana der Zukunft." *Una Sancta* 26 (1971) pp. 212-218.

--"The Mirage of the Future." *Teilhard Review* VIII, no., 2. London (June-1973) pp. 42-45.

________. "Der Mythos der Zukunft." in *Zukunft der Theologie. Theologie der Zukunft.* Vienna, Freiburg, Basel: Herder, 1971, pp. 17-26.

__________. "Philosophy of Religion in the Contemporary Encounter of Cultures." in R. Klibansky, ed., *Contemporary Philosophy: A Survey*. Firenze: La Nuova Editrice, 1971, pp. 221-242.

__________. "The Relation of the Gospels to Hindu Culture Religion." in D. G. Miller, D. Y. Hadidian, eds., *Jesus and Man's Hope*, Vol., II. Pittsburgh 1971, pp. 247-261.

__________. "The Rules of the Game in the Religious Encounter." *The Journal of Religious Studies*, III (Spring 1971) pp. 12-16.

--Also in *The Intrareligious Dialogue.* New York: The Paulist Press, 1978, pp. 25-37.

--Also in Gerald H. Anderson and Stransky, Thomas F., *Mission Trends No., 5: Faith Meets Faith: Lively Opinions from four Continents about Christian witness in the encounter with people of other faiths.* New York: Paulist Press, 1981. pp. 111-122.

--In French: "Quelques Présupposés à la Rencontre des Religions." *Rhythmes du Monde* 19 (1971-72) pp. 27-31.

--Also in *Diotima* 6 (1978) pp. 102-107.

1972

__________. "Témoignage et dialogue." *Archivo di Filosofia: La Testimonianza,* 40 (1972) pp. 367-388.

--"Witness and Dialogue", In *Myth, Fith and Hermeneutics: Cross Cultural Studies.* New York, Ramsey, Toronto 1979. pp. 231-256.

__________. "Some Aspects of Suffering and Sorrow in the Vedas." *Jeevadhara* II, no., 11 (Sept. - Oct., 1972) pp. 387-398.

--Also as: "Physical ailment." in *The Vedic Experience. Mantraman~jarí: An Anthology of the Vedas for Modern Man and Contemporary Celebration.* London: Darton, Longman and Todd, (1977) reprint, 1979, section I, part IV.

________. "Súnyatā and Pléróma: The Buddhist and Christian Response to the Human Predicament." *Religion and the Humanizing of Man: Plenary Addresses, International Congress of Learned Societies in the Field of Religion.* Canada: Waterloo, 1972, pp. 67-86.

--Also in *The Journal of Religious Studies* VI, no., 1 (Spring 1978) pp.16-34.

________. "Prolegomena to the Problem of the Universality of the Church." in J.B. Chethimattam, ed., *Unique and Universal: Fundamental Problems of an Indian Theology.* Bangalore: CSWR, Dharmaram 1972, pp. 155-163.

________. "The Theandric Vocation." *Monastic Studies* no., 8 (Spring-1972) pp. 67-74.

--In Portuguese: "A Vocaçāso Teândrica. Santidade: Afirmaçâo e Depojamento." *Grande Sinai* 33 (1979) pp. 205-213.

________. "`Super hanc petram': Due Principi Ecclesiologici: La Roccia e Le Chiavi." in *Legge e Vangelo: Discussione su una legge fundamentale per la Chiesa.* Paideia, 1972, PP. 135-145.

________. "The Meaning of Christ's name in the Universal Economy of Salvation." In *Documenta Missionalia 5: Evangelization Dialogue and Development.* Roma, 1972, pp. 195-218.

--And in *Salvation in Christ: Concreteness and Universality, the Supername.* Santa Barbara, 1972, pp. 16-41.

--Also in Joseph Patrapankal, ed., *Service and Salvation,* Bangalore: Theological Publications in India, 1973, pp. 235-263.

1973

________. "Tolérance, Idéologie et Mythe." *Archivo di Filosofia: Demitizzazione e Ideologia* 41 (1973) pp. 191-206.

--"Tolerance, Ideology and Myth", In *Myth, Fith and Hermeneutics: Cross Cultural Studies*. New York, Ramsey, Toronto, 1979, pp. 19-36.

--In Spanish: "Tolerancia, ideologíe y mytho." *Dialogos*, no., 79 (México) (January - February 1978) pp. 4-10.

__________. "The Category of Growth in Comparative religion: A Critical Self-examination. In *Harvard Theological Review* 66, No 1 (January 1973) pp. 113-140.

--Also in *The Intrareligious Dialogue* (New York: The Paulist Press, 1978) pp. 53-78.

__________. "Philosophy and Revolution: The Text, the Context and the Texture." *Philosophy East and West*, 3 (July, 1973) pp. 315-322.

__________. "Apologie de la Scolastique." *Diogène*, no., 83 (Jul-Sept., 1973) pp. 105-118.

__________. "Action and Contemplation as Categories of Religious Understanding." in *Main Currents in Modern Thought* 30 (Nov.-Dec., 1973) pp. 75-81.

--Also in *The Indian Journal of Theology* 15 (January-March 1976) pp. 17-29.

--Also in Y. Ibish and I. Masculescu, eds., *Contemplation and Action in World Religions. Selected Papers from the Rothok Chapel Colloquium on `Traditional Modes of Contemplation and Action'*. Seattle, London: A Rothko Chapel Book, 1978 pp. 85-104.

__________. "Monólogo con Vicente Fatone." In *Obras Completas de Vicente Fatone.* Vol., II, Buenos Aires, Suramericana, 1973, pp. 195-218.

__________. "Vāc in the S'ruti", In G. Gispert-Sauch, ed., *God's Word Among Men: Papers in Honour of Fr Joseph Putz, S.J., Fr J. Bayrt, S.J., J. Volckaert,S.J. and P. De Letter, S.J.* New Delhi: Vidiyajyoti Institute of Religious Studies, 1973, pp.

3-24.

1974

__________. "Le mythe comme Histoire Sacrée: Shunahshepa, un Mythe de la Condition Humaine." *Archivo di Filosofia: Il Sacro* 42 (1974) pp. 243-315.

--" S'una̤hs'pa. A Myth of the Human Condition," In *Myth, Fith and Hermeneutics: Cross Cultural Studies*. New York: The Paulist Press, 1979. pp. 97-184.

__________. "Have the `Religions' the *Monopoly* on Religion? Editorial." *Journal of Ecumenical Studies* XI, no., 3 (Summer 1974) pp. 515-517.

__________. "The Hindu Ecclesial Consciousness. Some Ecclesiological Reflections" *Jeevadhara* XXI (May-June, 1974) pp. 199 - 205.

__________. "The Silence of the Word: Non-dualistic Polarities." *Cross-Currents* 24 (Summer/Fall, 1974) pp. 154-171.

__________. "The Monk according to the Indian Sacred Scriptures." *Cistercian Studies* 9 (1974) pp. 253-255.

__________. "Toward a Typology of Time and Temporality in ancient Indian Tradition." *Philosophy of East and West* 24 (1974) pp. 161-164.

--Also in *Journal of Ecumenical Studies* XXIV (April, 1974) pp. 161-164.

1975

__________. "El presente tempiterno. Una apostilla a la historia de la salvación y a la teología de la liberación." in *Teología y Mundo Contemporáneo. Homenaje a K. Rahner en su 70 cumpleaños* Madrid 1974. Edited by A. Vargas Machuca. Madrid: Universidad Pontificia de Comillas, 1975, pp. 133-175.

In: "Le Temps Circulaire: Temporisation et Temporalité." *Archivo di Filosofia: Temporalità e Alienazione* 43 (1975) pp.

207-246.

________. "La Visione Cosmoteandrica: Il Senso religioso emergente del terzo millennio." in R. Caporale, ed., *Vecchi e Nuovi Dei: Studi e Riflessioni sul senso religioso emergente degli Atti del Il Simposio Internazionale sulla Credenza, organizzata dalla Fondazionale sulla Credenza, organizzata dalla Fondazione Giovanni Agnelli a Vienna 7-11 Gennaio 1975*. Valentino: Torino 1976, pp. 521-544.

--"The Cosmo theandric Vision: An Emerging consciousness for the Third Millennium A.D." *Vecchi e Neuoni Dei*, edited by R. Caporale. Torino: Valentino, 1976 pp. 521-544.

________. "The Contribution of Christian Monasticism in Asia to the Universal Church" *Cistercian Studies* 10, no., 2 (1975) pp. 73-74.

________. "Seed-Thoughts in Cross-Cultural Studies: Pensées dans la problématique pluriculturelle." *Monchanin* VIII, 3-5, cahier 50, (June- December, 1975) pp. 1-73.

________. "Astrologie." *Monchanin* VIII, 3-5, cahier 50 (Jun-Dec., 1975) pp. 71-73.

________. "Cross-Cultural Studies." *Monchanin* VIII, 3-5, cahier 50, (June- December, 1975) pp. 12-15.

________. "Le Dialogue." *Monchanin* VIII, 3-5, cahier 50, (June-December, 1975) pp. 47-50.

________. "Ecology from an Eastern Philosophical Perspective." *Monchanin* VIII, 3-5, cahier 50, (Jun-Dec., 1975) pp. 23-28.

________. "Education Religieuse dans une perspective inter-religieuse." *Monchanin* VIII, 3-5, cahier 50, (Jun-Dec., 1975) pp. 51-70.

________. "The Emerging Myth." Preface to Jacques Langlais, *Le Bouddha et les bouddhismes*, (Montreal 1975).
--Also in *Monchanin* VIII, 3-5, cahier 50, (Jun-Dec., 1975) pp. 8-11.

________. "L'Est et l'Ouest." *Monchanin* VIII, 3-5, cahier 50, (June-December, 1975) pp.37-45.

________. "Myth in Religious Phenomenology." *Monchanin* VIII, 3-5, cahier 50, (Jun-Dec., 1975) pp. 16-17.

________. "Mythos et Logos." *Monchanin* VIII, 3-5, cahier 50, (June-December, 1975) p. 46.

________. "Religious Education in an Inter-Faith Perspective." *Monchanin* VIII, 3-5, cahier 50, (Jun-Dec., 1975) pp. 23-32.

________. "Symbols and Reality. The 'Symbolic' Difference." *Monchanin* VIII, 3-5, cahier 50, (Jun-Dec., 1975) pp. 18-22.

________. "Inter-Religious Dialogue: Some Principles (Editorial)." *Journal of Ecumenical Studies* 12 (Summer 1975) pp. 407-409.

________. "Eastern and Western Ways of Thinking about God." (An interview between Panikkar and Walter T. Brennan, O.S.M), *Listening* 10 (Winter 1975) pp. 78-83.

________. "The Mutual Fecundation." (Foreword to) in T. Paul, ed., *The Emerging Culture in India*. Alwaye: Pontifical Institute of Theology and Philosophy, 1975, pp. 9-11.

________. "Singularity and Individuality. The Double Principle of Individuation." *Revue Internationale de Philosophie*, XXIX, no., 111-112, fasc. 1-2 (1975) pp. 141-166.

________. "Some Notes on Syncretism and Eclecticism related to the growth of human consciousness." in B.A. Pearson, ed., *Religious Syncretism in Antiquity. Essays in conversation with Geo. Widengren* (Montana 1975) pp. 47-62.

________. "Temps et Histoire dans la Tradition de l'Inde:" *Les Cultures et les Temps*. -- UNESCO-- Paris: Payot, 1975, pp. 73-101.

________. "Verstehen als Überzeugtsein" in H.G. Gadamer and P. Vogler, *Neue Anthropologie*, Vol., 7 *Philosophische Anthropologie*, Zweiter teil. Stuttgart: Georg Thieme Verlag, 1975, pp. 132- 167.

1976

________. "La Sécularisation de l'herméneutique. Le Cas du Christ: Fils de l'Homme et Fils de Dieu." *Archivo di Filosofia: L'Ermaeneutica della Secolarizzazione*. 44 (Padua, cedam, 1976) pp. 213-248.

--In German: "Die Säkularisierung der Hermeneutik. Der Fall Christus: Menschensohn und Gottessohn," in *Kerygma und Mythos VI - 9: zum problem der Sékularisierung ; Mythos oder Wirklichkeit Verhängnis oder Verhei$ung?* (Von) E. Grassi, P Ricoeur etc. (Akteu des Colloquiums über "Die Hermeneutik der Säkularisierung" Roma, Januar 1976 unter dem vorsitz von Enrico castelli). Hamburg -Bergstedt: H. Reich, 1977, pp. 141-165.

________. "Prologue." in A.T. de Nicolas, *Avatar and the Humanization of Philosophy through the Bhagavad Gita*, New York: Nicolas Hays, Ltd, 1976. IX-XIII.

1977

________. "La Philosophie de la Religion devant le Pluralisme Philosophique et la Pluralité des religions." *Archivo di Filosofia: Pluralisme Philosophique et Pluralité des Religions*. 45 (Padua, cedam, 1977) pp. 193-201.

--an abridged form "Athens or Jerusalem? Philosophy or Religion." *Logos* 2 (University of Santa Clara 1981) pp. 21-39.

________. "Social Ministry and Ministry of Word and Worship." in Achútegui, pedro de , SJ, ed., *Asian Colloquium on ministries in the Church. Hong Kong February 27- March 5, 1977* (Manila 1977) pp. 256-274.

__________. "Man as a Ritual Being." *Chicago Studies* XVI, 1 (Spring- 1977) pp. 5-28.

--Also in *Indian Theological Studies* 16 (1979) pp 6-31.

__________. "The New Innocence" *Cross Currents* XXVII (Spring 1977) pp. 7-15.

__________. "Prospettive Cristiane in Asia" (Interview). *Mondo e Missione* (Jun.-Jul., 1977) pp. 398-399.

__________. "Alternatives to Modern Culture. Provisional Draft concerning the Feasibility of a UNESCO Major Project." in *Filosofia e Disinovlvimiento. I-II Atas da III Semana internacional de Filosofia realizada na Cida de Salvador Ba de 17 a 23 Julho de 1976* (Rio de Janeiro 1977) pp. 395-398.

--Also as: "Alternatives to Modern Culture." *Interculture-77 --- (Oct.-Dec., 1982)* pp. 2-4.

--"Alternatives to Modern Cultures." In *The Whole Earth Papers* (Voices from India), 1 (Winter 1978) pp. 58-61.

__________. "Creation and Nothingness. Creation: exnihilo sed non in nihilum. Nothingness: ad quem sed non a quo." *Theologiche Zeitschrift.* 33 (September- October 1977) pp. 344-352.

__________. "Colligite Fragmenta: For an Integration of Reality." in F.A. Eigo and S.E. Fittipaldi, eds., *From Alienation to At-Oneness. Proceedings of the Theology Institute of Villanova University.* Villanova: The Villanova University Press, 1977, pp. 19-91.

__________. "The Time of Death: the Death of Time. An Indian Reflection." *La réflexion sur la mort.* [Proceedings of the II Symposion International de Philosophie]. Athens: École libre de Philosophie `Pléton', 1977, pp. 102-121.

_________. "Eine unvollendete Symphonie." in G. Neske, ed., *Erinnerung on Martin Heidegger*. Pfullingen: NESKE, 1977, pp. 173-178.

_________. "Samdhya the Vedic prayer." *Indian Theological Studies* 14 (Bangalore 1977) pp. 22-38.

1978

_________. "Religion ou Politique: Y a-t-il une solution au problème de l'Occident?." *Archivo di Filosofia I nuovi Aspetti della dimitizzazione: Religione e Politica*. 46 (Padua: cedam, 1976) pp. 73-82.

--"Non dualistic Relation between Religion and Politics." *Religion and Society* XXV (Sept., 1978) pp. 53-63.

_________. "The Bostonian Verities: A comment on the Boston Affirmations.'" *Andover Newton Quarterly* XVIII, 3 (January 1978) pp. 145-153.

_________. "Man and his Spirituality." *Forum for Correspondence and Contact* 9 (Jan., 1978) pp. 58-61.

_________. "The Texture of a Text: in Response to Paul Ricoeur." *Point of Contact*. (April-May, 1978) pp. 51-64.

_________. "The Vitality and Role of Indian Philosophy Today." *Indian Philosophical Quarterly* 5 (July, 1978) pp. 673-692.

_________. "Philosophy as Life-Style." in A. Mercier and M. Svilar, eds., *Philosophers on their own Work*. Vol., IV, Berne: Peter Lang, 1978, pp. 193-228.

_________. "Time and Sacrifice. The Sacrifice of Time and the Ritual of Modernity." in J.T. Fraser, N. Lawrence and D. Park, eds., *The Study of Time III., Proceedings of the III Conference of the International Society for the Study of Time, Alpbad - Austria* (Berlin 1978) pp. 683-725.

_________. "Hermeneutics of Comparative Religion: Paradigms and Models." *The Journal of Religious Studies* VI, 1

(Spring) 1978. pp. 38-51.

--Also in *Journal of Dharma* V, 1 (Jan-Mar., 1980) pp. 38-51.

__________. "`Gedankenfreie' Meditation oder seinserfullte Gelassenheit?" In *Munen Muso~. Ungegenständliche Meditation.* [Festschrift fur Hugo M. Enomiya-Lassalle, S.J.zum 80. Geburtstag] Edited by G. Stachel. Mainz Grünewald, 1978, pp. 309-316.

__________. "The Rhetoric of interreligious dialogue p. 367-380 *Jeevadhara* 8(Kottayam 1978) pp. 367-380.

1979

__________. "*Rtatattva*: A Preface to a Hindu-Christian Theology." IX, *Jeevadhara* (Jan-Feb., 1979) pp. 6-63.

__________. "The Myth of Pluralism: The Tower of Babel - A Meditation on Non-Violence." *Cross-Currents* 29 (Summer, 1979) pp. 197-230.

__________. "Some Words instead of a Response." *Cross-Currents* 29, (Summer 1979) pp. 193-196.

__________. "Response to Harold Coward." *Cross Currents* 29 (Summer 1979) pp. 190-192.

__________. "La Religión del Futuro o la Crisis del concepto de religión: La religiosidad Humana." *Civiltà delle Macchine.* (Roma) XXVII, no., 4-6 (Lug-Dic., 1979) pp. 82-90.

__________. "Religione e Cultura: Prolegomeni." (Conversazione di Francesco d'Arcais con Raimundo Panikkar e Milan Simcic^)." *Civiltá delle Macchine.* Roma, XXVII, no., 4-6 (Lug-Dic.,) 1979, pp. 6-16.

__________. "Common Patterns of Eastern and Western Scholasticism." in *Actos del V Congreso Internacional de Filosofía Medieval.* Vol., II, Madrid: Editora Nacional, 1979, pp. 1059-1066.

__________. "Hinduism, Church and," *New Catholic Encyclopedia*, Vol., XVII *Supplement: Change in the*

Church. Edited by the Catholic University of America, Washington DC & New York: Book Company, 1979, pp. 257-259.

__________. "Reflexoes Interculturais sobre a Filosofia da Linguagem." *Presença Filosófica*, V, 2. Raio da Janeiro (Abril-Junho, 1979) pp. 14-23.

__________. "You are Witnesses of This: A Symposium." Santa Cruz: Holy Trinity Monastery, 1979. A Dialogue with B. Barnhart and D. Nicholl. 45 pp.

__________. Preface to *Theresa of Avila: The Interior Castle*, trans. by Kieran Kavanaugh o.c.d and Otilio Rodriguez o.c.d., New York: Paulist Press, 1979, pp. xi-xix.

1980

__________. "Words and Terms." in *Existenza, Mito Ermeneutica (Scritti per Enrico Castelli)* Vol., II. Edited by M. Olivetti. (*Archivo di Filosofia*) Padova: CEDAM, 1980, pp. 117-133.

__________. "Some Theses on Philosophy and Liberation." *Monchanin* 13 (July - September 1980) pp. 39-40.

__________. "Chronicles." *Journal of Dharma* V (Oct-Dec., 1980) pp. 415-424.

__________. "Aporias in the Comparative Philosophy of Religion." *Man and World*. 13, 3-4 (1980) pp. 357-383.

__________. "A Philosophy of Liberation." Book Review of *Filosophia de la Liberación*, by Enrique Dussel, Mexico: Editoriar Edicol, S.A. 1977, in *Cross Currents* XXX, Winter 1980-81, pp.454-455.

__________. "Che accade all'uomo quando muore?" *Bozze*, 80 (1980) pp. 117- 136.

1981

__________. "Indian Theology: A Theological Mutation." in M. Amaladass, T.K. John, G. Gispert-Sauch, eds., *Theologizing* in India. *Selection of Papers presented at the Seminar held at Pune on October 26-30, 1978* (Bangalore 1981) pp. 23-42

__________. "L'eau et la Mort. Réflexion interculturelle sur une métaphore." *Archivio di Filosofia: Filosofia e Religione di fronte alla Morte.* 49 (1981) pp. 481-502.

__________. "Letter to friends of Salvador de Bahìa." *Monchanin* 70 (Jan-Mar., 1981) pp. 37-43.

__________. "Man and Religion: a Dialogue with Panikkar." [A Dialogue between Panikkar and Koothottil]. *Jeevadhara* XI (Jan-Feb., 1981) pp. 5-32.

__________. "Inde et Europe, Indiens et Chrétiens: Danser ensemble." (Dialogue entre R.Panikkar and G.Deleury), *Foi et Solidarité des Peuples* Document 5 [Dialogue entre R. Panikkar and G. Deleury] (Avril-1981) pp. 2-45.

__________. "The Contemplative Mood: A Challenge to Modernity." *Cross-Currents* XXXI, 3 (Fall, 1981) pp. 261-272.

__________. "Is History the Measure of Man? Three Kairological Moments of Human Consciousness." *The Teilhard Review.* 16, 1&2 (London, 1981) pp. 39-45.

__________. "Is there Place for the *Temple* in the Modern City?" *Changing Perception of Development Problems.* Edited by R.P. Misra and M.Honjo. Nagoya, Japan: United Nations Centre for regional Development; Singapore: Maruzen Asia, 1981, pp. 275-288.

__________. "Per una cultura transculturale del Simbolo." in C. Brutti, F. Scotti, eds., *Simbolo e Simbolizzazione* [Quaderni di Psicoterapia infantile 5] (Roma 1981) pp. 53-91.

__________. `Rejoinds' the Reviews of *Myth, Faith and Hermeneutics*, given by S. Fttipaldi, P. Knitter, K. Mitra, J. Ramish, in *Horizons* (CTS) 8 (Spring 1981) pp. 122-131)., in *Horizons* 8 (Spring 1981) pp. 132-134.

1982

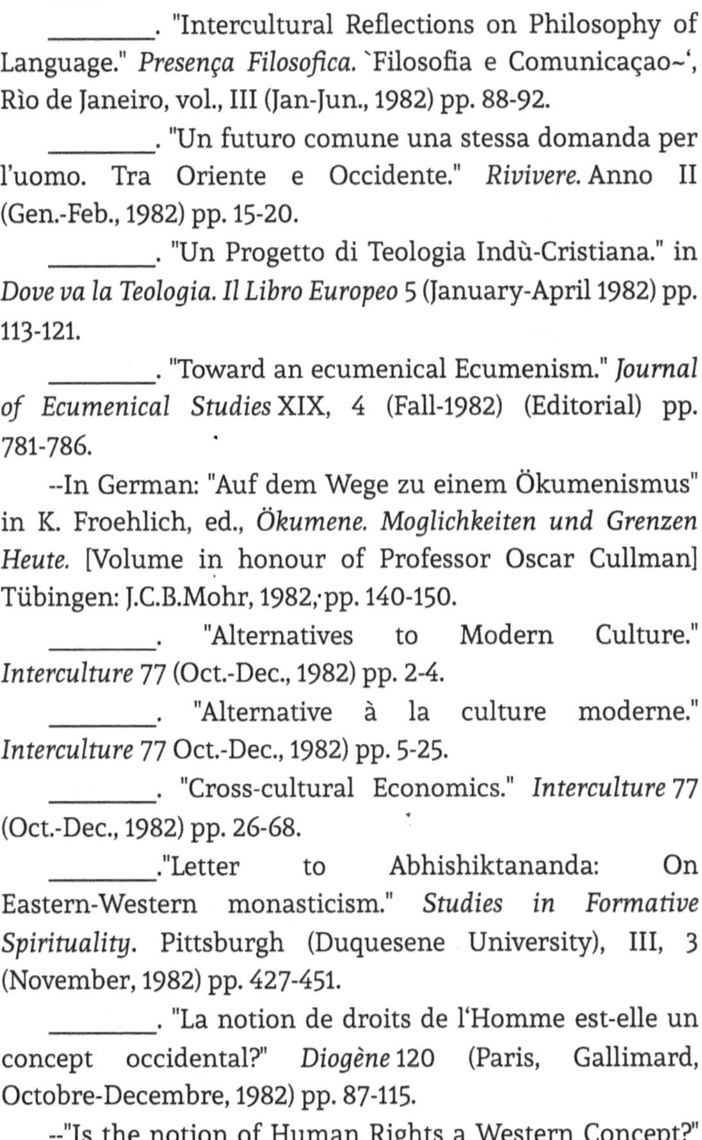

__________. "Intercultural Reflections on Philosophy of Language." *Presença Filosofica.* `Filosofia e Comunicaçao~`, Rìo de Janeiro, vol., III (Jan-Jun., 1982) pp. 88-92.

__________. "Un futuro comune una stessa domanda per l'uomo. Tra Oriente e Occidente." *Rivivere.* Anno II (Gen.-Feb., 1982) pp. 15-20.

__________. "Un Progetto di Teologia Indù-Cristiana." in *Dove va la Teologia. Il Libro Europeo* 5 (January-April 1982) pp. 113-121.

__________. "Toward an ecumenical Ecumenism." *Journal of Ecumenical Studies* XIX, 4 (Fall-1982) (Editorial) pp. 781-786.

--In German: "Auf dem Wege zu einem Ökumenismus" in K. Froehlich, ed., *Ökumene. Moglichkeiten und Grenzen Heute.* [Volume in honour of Professor Oscar Cullman] Tübingen: J.C.B.Mohr, 1982, pp. 140-150.

__________. "Alternatives to Modern Culture." *Interculture* 77 (Oct.-Dec., 1982) pp. 2-4.

__________. "Alternative à la culture moderne." *Interculture* 77 Oct.-Dec., 1982) pp. 5-25.

__________. "Cross-cultural Economics." *Interculture* 77 (Oct.-Dec., 1982) pp. 26-68.

__________. "Letter to Abhishiktananda: On Eastern-Western monasticism." *Studies in Formative Spirituality.* Pittsburgh (Duquesene University), III, 3 (November, 1982) pp. 427-451.

__________. "La notion de droits de l'Homme est-elle un concept occidental?" *Diogène* 120 (Paris, Gallimard, Octobre-Decembre, 1982) pp. 87-115.

--"Is the notion of Human Rights a Western Concept?" *Diogène*, no., 120 (Winter 1982) pp. 75-102.

--In Spanish: "?Es occidental el concepto de los derechos humanos?" *Diogènes* (Mexico) (Winter 1982) pp. 85-116.

___________. "El Círculo Sólo si el tiempo es circular vale la pena romperlo" in *Octavio Paz* (Madrid, Taurus), 1982, pp. 215-222.

___________. "à l'encontre de deu anthropologies." Preface to *Vers una sexologia de la Religió*, by E. Aguilar. Barcelona (Edicions 62), 1982, pp. 7-10.

___________. "Sobre l'hinduisme: i el cristianismo: Una questión de vida crisiana." *Questions de vida cristiana.* Montserrat: Publicaciones de la Abadía de Montserrat, 1982, pp. 54-72.

___________. "The Intrareligious Dialogue." *Contemporary American Theologies*, II: A Book of Readings Ed. by Deane Williams Ferm. New York: The Seabury Press, 1982, pp. 356-366.

1983

___________. "The Machine in Ancient Buddhist Prophecy." *Epiphany*, 4, (Fall, 1983) pp. 120-123.

___________. "The Global Village." *The Tablet* 9 (July, 1983) pp. 649-650.

--also "Let us stop Speaking about `the Global Village'." *Interculture* 16 (Oct-Dec., 1983) pp. 34-36.

___________. "The End of History: The Threefold Structure of Human Time-Consciousness." *Teilhard and the unity of Knowledge.* Edited by Thomas M. King and James F. Salamon. New York: Paulist Press, 1983, pp. 83-141.

--Italian "La fine della storia: la triplice struttura della conscienza umana del tempo." *Quaderni di psicoterapia infantile: Tempo e Psicoanalisi.* Perugia, Borla, 1984, pp. 16-109.

________. "La vocation humaine est fondamentalement religieuse? Recontre avec R. Panikkar." *Nouveau Dialogue* (SIF), no., 51 (Sept., 1983) pp. 3 - 11.

________. "Interview." [R.Panikkar interviewed by Peter Reinhart]. *Epiphany* 3 (Summer, 1983) pp. 2-31.

________. "Prefazione." *Liberaci dal male. Male e vie di liberazione nelle Religioni.* Bologna: La Nuova Stampa, 1983, pp. 7-19.

________. "Regard sur l'Avenir de la Mission." *Bulletin de l'entraide Missionnaire* 25 (September 1983) pp. 137-147.

1984

________. "The Cosmotheandric Intuition." *Jeevadhara* -79 (Jan. 1984) pp. 27-35.

________. "L'atteggiamento contemplativo: una sfida per la modernitá" in *Contemplazione e ricerca spirituale nella societá se colarizzata. La proposta di Merton e Maritaian.* Milano: Massimo, 1984, pp. 37-52.

________. "Religione e filosofie dell'Oriente." *Nouva Secondaria* - 8. Brecia (La Scuola), April, 1984, p. 41.

________. "A Dialogue on Human Rights." *Interculture* - 83 (April-June, 1984) pp. 78-82.

________. "Response Regarding Media, Electioneering and Human Values." *Forum* 14 (June, 1984) pp. 46-47.

________. "The Dialogical Dialogue". In *The World's Religious Traditions: Current Perspectives in Religious Studies. Essays in Honour of Wilfred Cantwell Smith.* Edited by Frank Whaling. Edinburgh: T. & T. Clark., 1984, pp. 61-72.

________. "La pau política com a objectiù religiós." *Questions de Vida Cristiana.* 121, Montserrat: Publicacions de l'Abadia de Montserrat, 1984, pp. 83-84.

________. "La Interpellaciò del'Asia al Cristianisme." *Theologia i Vida.*Barcelona: Editorial Claret, 1984, pp. 81-93.

__________. "Quelques thèses supplémentaires sur la technologie". In *Philosophie et technique*, edited by André Mercier. Berne and Paris: Institut International de Philosophie, 1984, pp. 61-72.

__________. "Religious Pluralism: The Metaphysical Challenge". In *Religious Pluralism*. Notre Dame: Notre Dame University Press, 1984, pp. 97-115.

__________. "Sein und Nichts: Fragender Durchblick auf die entfaltete Problematik". In *Sein und Nichts in der Abendländischen Mystik*, edited by Walter Strolz. Freiburg, Basel, Wien: Herder, 1984, pp. 107-123.

__________. "L'émancipation de la théologie". In *Interculture* 85 (Octobre-Decembre 1984) pp. 22-37.

__________. "The Dream of an Indian Ecclesiology". In *Searching for an Indian Ecclesiology*, edited by Indian Theological Association, Bangalore: Asian Trading Corporation, 1984, pp. 24-54.

__________. "The Destiny of Technological Civilization: An Ancient Buddhist Legend: Romavisaya". In *Alternatives. A Journal of World Policy.* X (Fall, 1984) pp. 237 -253.

__________. "The Catholic Experience Towards a Theoanthropocosmic Vision". In *Was ist die Natur*, Edited by the Institut für Interkulturelle Forschung in Japan, Kyoto. Japan: Verlag Hozokan, 1984, pp. 83 -107.

__________. "La grazia di Babele". In *Bozze* 84 (1984) Rome.

1985

__________. "Religion and Politics: The Western Dilemma". In *Religion and Politics in the Modern World*, edited by Peter H. Merkl and Ninian Smart, New York and London: New York University Press, 1985, pp. 44-90.

__________. "Una perspectiva intercultural de la `teología de la liberación'" In *El Pais* Madrid (February 11, 1985) pp.

9-10.

__________. "Global Perspectives: Spiritualities in Interaction." *Journal of Dharma* 10 (January- March 1985) pp. 6-17.

__________. "Foreword". In *Heat and Sacrifice in the Vedas*, by UM*ā*-Marina Vesci. Delhi, Varanasi, Patna, Madras: Motilal Banarsidass, 1985, pp. xi -xvii.

__________. "Der Mensch, ein trinitarisches Mysterium". In *Die Verantwortung des Menschen für eine bewohnbere Welt im Christentum, Hinduismus und Buddhismus.* Edited by R. Panikkar and W. Strolz, Freiburg: Herder, 1985, pp. 147 -150.

__________. "Dios en las Religiones". In *Misión Abierta.*[Special volume dedicated to the V Congress of Theology: Madrid-Septiembre -1985]. Madrid (1985) Nrs.5-6, pp. 85 - 102.

__________. "Présentation. Un traité de spiritualité." Préface to *La voie Jaina: histoire, spiritualité, vie des ascètes pèlerins de l'Inde,* by N. Shanta. Paris: O.E.I.L. --Collection les deux rives-- 1985, pp. 17-32.

__________. "Qué vol dir avui confessar-se cristiá?". In *Questions de vida cristiana,* Nr. 128 - 129. Montserrat: Publications de l'Abadia de Montserrat, 1985, pp. 86-111.

__________. "Foreword." to *The Vision of Cosmic Order in the Vedas,* by Jeanine Miller. London: Routledge & Kegan Paul, 1985, pp.xi- xix.

__________. "Present-Day University Education and World Cultures". In *Interculture,* (Summer 1985) pp. 2-15.

__________. "Cultural Disarmament." [Foreword to the Summary of a research conducted by R. Rapp under the guidance of R. Panikkar in UCSB - 1984]. In *Interculture,* (Fall, 1985) p. 14.

________. "The Sermon on the mount of intrareligious Dialogue." (Editorial) in *Journal of Ecumenical Studies* XXII (Fall, 1985) p. 773.

1986

________. "Some Thesis on Technology". In *Logos* 7 (1986) pp. 115-124.

________. "La Montée vers le Fond." Préface a H. Le Saux (Abhishitananda) *La Montée Au Fond Du Coeur Le journal intime du moine chrétien-sannyāsi hindou.* Paris: O.E.I.L., Les Deux Rives.

________. "The Jesus Debate. Cross-Cultural Considerations". [Review of *The Jesus Debate* by William Thompson] In *The Ecumenist*, 24, (Jul-Aug., 1986) pp. 72-76.

________. "Un Tirano Anonimo" i "La Torre di Babele." *L'Altrapagina*, no., 6 (Giugno 1986) p. 6.

________. "The Threefold Linguistic Intrasubjectivity." *Archivio Di Filosofia* LIV, no., 1-3 (1986) pp. 593-606.

________. "The Pope and the Angels." *The Tablet* 240, no., 7632 (Oct., 1986) p. 1098.

________. "Medicina y Religión." *Jano*, no., 737 (Jul., 1986) pp. 12-48.

________. "La dialéctica de la razón armada." (Entrevista) *Concordia*, 9 (1986), pp. 68-89.

1987

________. "The Challenge of Religious Studies to the Issues of our Times". Foreword to Scott Eastham, *Nucleus: Reconnecting Science and Religion in the Nuclear Age.* Beard and Co., 1987, pp. xiii- xxxviii.

________. "Letter to a Young Monk". *Living Prayer* (Nov.-Dec., 1987) pp.11-14.

________. "El Somni d'una Església India." *Questions de Vida Cristiana* 131-132 (Montserrat 1987) pp. 174-199.

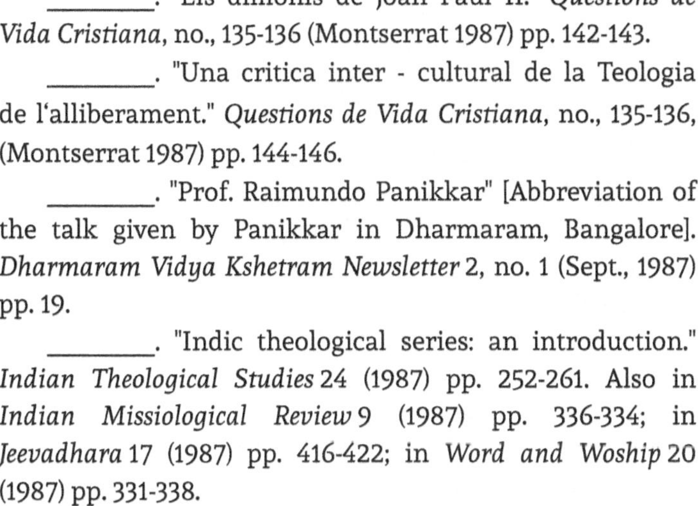

__________. "Els dimonis de Joan Paul II." *Questions de Vida Cristiana*, no., 135-136 (Montserrat 1987) pp. 142-143.

__________. "Una critica inter - cultural de la Teologia de l'alliberament." *Questions de Vida Cristiana*, no., 135-136, (Montserrat 1987) pp. 144-146.

__________. "Prof. Raimundo Panikkar" [Abbreviation of the talk given by Panikkar in Dharmaram, Bangalore]. *Dharmaram Vidya Kshetram Newsletter* 2, no. 1 (Sept., 1987) pp. 19.

__________. "Indic theological series: an introduction." *Indian Theological Studies* 24 (1987) pp. 252-261. Also in *Indian Missiological Review* 9 (1987) pp. 336-334; in *Jeevadhara* 17 (1987) pp. 416-422; in *Word and Woship* 20 (1987) pp. 331-338.

B. *Secondary Sources*: *The Literature Referring to Panikkar*

1. Books and Articles

BAHR, ANN MARIE. "Ecumenical Events." [Summary of the Conference `Toward a Universal Theology of Religion' held at Temple University, October 17-19, 1984] *Journal of Ecumenical Studies* 22 (Winter 1984) pp. 194-198.

BALWANT, PARADKAR. "The Christian Encounter with men of other faiths." *Religion and Society*, XIV, no., 2.

BIELAWSKI, MACIEJ. "Panikkar: His Life and His Works," Campo Dei Fiori, 2018.

CAPPS, WALTER H., "Toward a Christian theology of the World's Religions." *Cross Currents* 29 (Summer 1979) pp. 156-168, 182.

CHAUMEIL M.J., "Madame Daniélou en son temps." *Cahiers de Neuilly* (January, 1967) pp. 5-63.

CHETHIMATTAM, J.B. CMI. "Indian Approaches to Christology: R. Panikker's approach to Christology." *The*

Indian Journal of Theology 23 (1974) pp. 219-222.

CLEMENT OLIVIER, "Rencontre." *Axes* 7 (1974-1975) pp. 167-172.

CRACKNELL, KENNETH. "Christianity and Religious Pluralism: The Ethics of Interfaith relations. *Christian Jewish Relations*, 18, no., 2 (June, 1985) pp. 40-58.

COUSINS, EWERT H., "Introduction: The Panikkar Symposium at Santa Barbara." *Cross Currents* 29 (Summer 1979) pp. 131-134, 140.

COUSINS, EWERT H., "Raimundo Panikkar and the Christian systematic theology of the future." *Cross Currents* 29 (Summer 1979) pp. 141-155.

COWARD, HAROLD G., "Panikker's Approach to Interreligious Dialogue." *Cross Currents* 29 (Summer 1979) pp. 183-189. 192.

CULLMANN OSCAR, "Rencontre." *Axes* 7 (1974-1975) pp. 173-175.

DANKFRIED, REETZ. "Raymond Panikkar's theology of religions." *Religion and Society* XV, no., 3 (1968) pp. 46-54.

D'COSTA, GAVIN. "Karl Rahner's anonymous Christian: a reappraisal." *Modern Theology* 1 (January 1985) pp. 131-148.

DE GANDILLAC, MAURICE. "Jean Daniélou et'Dieu Vivant'." *Axes* 7 (1974 - 1975) pp. 125-130.

DEVADAS, NALINI. "The Theandrism of Raimundo Panikkar and Trinitarian Parallels in Modern Hindu Thought." *Journal of Ecumenical Studies* 17 (1980) pp. 606-620.

D'SA, FRANCIS. "Myth, History and Cosmos." *Jeevadhara* XIV, no., 79 (1984) pp. 7-26.

D'Sa, Francis X. "Panikkar, Raimon (1918-2010)." *ACPI Encyclopedia of Philosophy*. Ed. Johnson J. Puthenpurackal. Bangalore: ATC 2010.

D'SOUZA, JEROME, S.J. "Exploding the Myth of East and West." *Worldmission* 9, no., 1 (1958) pp. 23-32.

DUPUIS, J. "The presence of Christ in Hinduism." *Clergy Monthly*, 34, pp.141-148.

__________. "Trinity and World Religions: Some Reflections on a Recent Book." *Clergy Monthly*, 35 (Feb., 1971) pp. 77-80.

__________. *Jesus Christ and His Spirit*. Bangalore: Theological Publications in India, 1977.

EMPRAYIL, THOMAS, V.C. *The Emerging Theology of Religions: The Contribution of the Catholic Church in India*. India: Vincentian Publications, 1980.

FRIES, HEINRICH. "Heil im Hinduismus." *In Heil in den Religionen und im Christentum*, Heinrich Fries; J. Brosseder; H. Bürkle; F. Köster; and F. Wolfinger. St. Ottilien: Eos Verlag Erzabtei, 1982, pp. 30-53.

GISPERT-SAUCH, G. "Raimon Panikkar." *Vidyajyoti: Journal of Theological Reflection*, December 2010.

GOMES, FELIPE, sj. "The Uniqueness and Universality of Christ." *East Asian Pastoral Review* XX, no., 1 (1983) pp. 4-30.

GOULET, JACQUES. "The Ultimate Indiscernibility of Faith." *African Ecclesial Review* 22 (Oct. 1980) pp. 288-293.

GRIFFITHS, BEDE. *Christ in India: Essays Towards a Hindu Christian Dialogue*. Bangalore: Asian Trading Corporation, 1986.

HARDON, JOHN A. *Gott in den Religionen der Welt*, München: Rex-Verlag Luzern, 1967.

HERBSTRITH, WALTRAUD. *Begegnung mit Indien: und einem seiner gro$en christlichen Pioniere Kuriackos Elias Chavara*. Trier: Johann Josef Zimmer Verlag, 1969.

JOSEP-IGNASI Saranyan Raimon Panikkar: a propósito de una biografía (in: *Studia et Documenta* 2017, Vol. 11, p. 323-348).

KAROKARAN, ANTO. *Evangelization and diakonia: A Study in the Evangelization and diakonia: A Study in the Indian Perspective.* Dharmaram Publications, Bangalore 1978 pp. 140-158; 206-211.

KNITTER, PAUL F. "Theocentric Christology", *Theology Today* 40 (July 1983) pp. 130-149.

___________. *No Other Name? A Critical Survey of Christian Attitudes toward the World Religions.* London: SCM Press, 1985, pp. 145-167.

KOMULAINEN. JYRI *An Emerging Cosmotheandric Religion?: Raimon Panikkar's Pluralistic Theology Of Religions* .Boston: Brill Academic Publishers, 2005.

KOOTHOTIL, ABRAHAM. "Man and Religion: A Dialogue with Panikkar." *Jeevadhara* 11 (1981) pp. 5-43.

KÜNG, HANS. *Theologie im Aufbruch.* München: Piper 1987.

LUKE, K. "Mythical Language, its Origin and Significance." *Jeevadhara* XIV, no., 79 (1984) pp. 36-51.

MACQUARRIE, JOHN. "Some Problems of Modern Christology" *Jeevadhara.* 23 (1974) pp. 155-175.

MENACHERRY, CHERIYAN. *Christ: The Mystery in History: A Critical Study on the Christology of Raymond Panikkar.* Peter Lang Publ Inc. (June 1996)

MILLER, JEANINE. *The Vision of Cosmic Order in the Vedas.* Foreword by Raimundo Panikkar. London: Routledge & Kegan Paul, 1985.

MITRA KANA, *Catholicism and Hinduism. A Vedantic Investigation of Raimundo Panikkar's Attempt at Bridge Building* (Unpublished doctoral thesis) (Temple University

1980).

MOLINARIO F., "L'evangelizzazione delle Culture e delle Religioni nella Esperienza e negli Scritti di Raymond Panikkar." *Testimonianza* 15 (1977) pp. 314-341.

MOOKENTHOTTAM, ANTONY M.S.F.S. *Indian Theological Tendencies: Approaches and Problems for Further Research as Seen in the Works of Some Leading Indian Theologians.* Frankfurt: Peter Lang, 1978.

__________. *Towards a Theology in the Indian Context.* Bangalore: Asian Trading Corporation, 1980.

MORETA, IGNASI. "Raimon Panikkar: an intense life, intercultural thought," in Barcelona Metropolis,
https://www.barcelona.cat/bcnmetropolis/2007-2017/en/

MULDER, D.C., "Rymond Panikkar's Dialog Met Het Hindoeìsme'." *Gereformeers Theologisch Tiydschrift* (August, 1969) pp. 186-198.

MUNDADAN, A.M. "Hindu-Christian Dialogue: Past Twenty Five Years." (A Survey of Indian Christian Literature) *Jeevadhara*, XI (1981) pp. 375-394.

NÉDONCELLE, MAURICE. "Philosophie de la Religion." in *La Philosophie Contemporaine.* Edited by Raymond Klibansky. Firenz: La Nuova Italia Editrice 1971, pp. 170-213.

NELSON, BENJAMIN. "A New Science of Civilizational analysis: A Tribute to Panikkar." *Cross Currents* 29 (Summer 1979) pp. 135-140.

NEUMAN MARTIN, "New Approaches for Benedictine Studies: A Review Essay of Raimundo Panikkar's *Blessed Simplicity.*" *The American Benedictine Review* 35 (June 1984) pp. 128-145.

PANDIKATTU, KURUVILLA Christian Advaita as the Hermeneutic Key to Bede Griffiths' Understanding of Interreligious Dialogue. Ph D Thesis in Theology, Innsbruck: Univ of Innsbruck, 1996. (Chapter 2 on Panikkar)

PANIKKAR, R., Curriculum Vitae. "List of Books and Selected Articles." Santa Barbara 1984.

PANUNZIO, S., "Christus und Indian. Jesus und Wir." (Eigespräch in Rom über *'Māyā* e Apocalisse' von Raimundo Panikkar) Interventions by Panunzio, Sforza, Vereno, Trevisonno, Fortunato and Panikkar, *Kairos* (1968) pp. 115-132.

PARAPPALLY, JACOB *Emerging Trends in Indian Christology: A Critical Study of the Development, Context and Contemporary Catholic Attempts of R.Panikkar and S.Kappen to Articulate a Relevant Christology in Indian Context.* (1992) by, MSFS,

PARRINDER, GEOFFREY. *Avatar and Incarnation.* New York: Oxford University Press, 1982.

OHM, THOMAS. *Asiens Nein und Ja zum westlichen Christentum.* Zweit, neu bearbeitet Auflage. Münhen: Kösel-Verlag, 1960.

________. "Geben Sie uns ein Christusbuch." *Der Chrisliche Sonntag,* XIII, no., 39 (1961).

PIRYNS, ERNEST D. "Current Roman Catholic Views of other Religions." *Missionalia* 13 (August 1985) pp. 55-62.

PODGORSKI, FRANK. "Contemplatio: The Cosmotheandric insight of Raimundo Panikkar." *Logos* 2, 1981, pp. 41-57.

RAJ, ANTHONY SAVARI. A *New Hermeneutic of Reality: Raimon Panikkar's Cosmotheandric Vision.* Peter Lang Publishing (August 1998)

"RAYMOND PANIKKAR (Close-up)." *Jubilee* 13 (Oct. 1965) pp. 24-25.

REETZ, D. "Raymond Panikkar's Theology of Religions." *Religion and Society* 15, no.,3 (1968) pp. 32-55.

ROBINSON, JOHN A.T. *Truth is Two-Eyed*, London: SCM Press, 1979.

SALDANHA, CHRYS. *Divine Pedagogy. A Patristic View of Non-Christian Religions* (Biblioteca di Scienze Religiose 57. Rome 1984.

SALTER, PETER. "Three Types of Reasoning in Religion", *Journal of American Academy of Religion* 49, no., 1 (1982) pp. 17-34.

__________. "Hindu and Christian Symbols in the work of R. Panikkar." *Cross Currents* 29 (1979) pp. 169-182.

SMET, ROBERT. *Essai sur la pensée de Raimundo Panikkar, une contribution indienne à la théologie des religions et à la Christologie.* Louvain-la-Neuve: Centre d'Histoire des Religions, 1981.

__________. *Le Problème d'une théologie Hindoue-Chrétienne selon Raymond Panikkar.* Louvain-La-Neuve: Centre d'Histoire des Religions, 1983.

VALLUVASSERY, CLEMENT. *Christus im Kontext und Kontext in Christus: Chalcedon und indische Christologie bei Raimon Panikkar und Samuel Rayan.* Münster: LIT Verlag. 2001.

VATTAKERIL, PETER. *Dialogue with men of other faiths: its theological implications. A critical study of Raimundo Panikkar.* (Excerpta ex dissertation ad Doctoratum in Facultatae Theologiae Pontificiae Universitatis Gregorianae). Roma: Pontificia Universitas Gregorianum, 1986.

VELIATH, DOMINIC. *Understanding of Religions: Jean Daniélou and Raimundo Panikkar, A Study in Contrast.* Bangalore: Kristujoyti College, 1981.

2. Book Reviews

ARGAUD, JACKY. Review of *Le Dialogue Intrareligieux*, by Panikkar, in *Etudes Theologiques et Religieuses*, 61, no., 3 (1986) pp. 468-469.

BARNES, M. Review of *Myth, Faith and Hermeneutics*, by Panikkar, in *Month*, 10 (Summer 1977) p. 319.

BHATTACHARYA, C. Review of *The Intra-Religious Dialogue*, by Panikkar, in *Religious Education* 74 (Nov-Dec., 1979) pp. 679-680.

BONNICHON, A. *Review of Lettre sur l'Inde*, by Panikkar, in *Etudes*, 320 (March 1964) p. 416.

BRENNAN, E. Review of *Myth, Faith and Hermeneutics*, by Panikkar, in *Journal of Ecumenical Studies*, 18 (Summer 1981) pp. 505-506.

CAMPBELL, T. Review of *The Intra-Religious Dialogue*, by Panikkar, in *Sisters Today*, 50 (April 1979) p. 590.

CHARLES, JOHN. Bro. Review of *Blessed Simplicity: The Monk as Universal Archetype*, by Panikkar, in *Spiritual Life*, 29 (Summer 1983) p. 115.

CHETHIMATTAM, J. Review of *The Vedic Experience: Mantramanjari*, by R. Panikkar, in *Thought*, 54 (Dec., 1979) p. 432.

CORBISHLEY, T. Review of *Worship and Secular Man*, by Panikkar, in *Month* 6 (July, 1973) p. 250.

COWARD, HAROLD. Review of *Myth, Faith and Hermeneutics*, by Panikkar, in *Journal of American Academy of Religion*, 49 (Dec., 1981) pp. 728-729.

__________. Review of *The Unknown Christ of Hinduism: Towards An Ecumenical Christophany,* by Panikkar, in *Religious Studies Bulletin*, 4 (Jan. 1984) pp. 33-35

CRACKNELL, K. Review of *Myth, Faith and Hermeneutics*, by Panikkar, in *Theology*, 85 (March 1982) pp.

144-145.

DEADY, E. Review of *Worship and Secular Man*, by Panikkar, in *Living Light*, 11 (Summer 1974) pp. 319-320.

DE LETTER, P. Review of *Kultmysterium in Hinduismus und Christentum: Ein Beitrag zur vergleichenden Religionstheololgie,* by Panikkar, in *The Clergy Monthly* (Supplement to) XXIX (Sept., 1965) pp. 301-302.

--Also in *Theologische Revue,* nr. 6 (1967) pp. 370-378.

DE NICHOLÅS, A. Review of *Blessed Simplicity: The Monk as Universal Archetype,* by Panikkar, in *Cross Currents,* 32 (Winter 1982-1983) pp. 470-473.

DEVINE, G. Review of *Worship and Secular Man,* by Panikkar, in *Cross Currents,* 23 (Summer 1973) pp. 211-212.

DHAVAMONY, M. Review of *The Unknown Christ of Hinduism,* by R. Panikkar, in *The Heythrop Journal,* 6 (Oct., 1986) pp. 479-481.

DUPUIS, J., Review of *The Unknown Christ of Hinduism,* by R. Panikkar, in *The Clergy Monthly* (Supplement to) XXIX (Sept., 1965) pp. 278-283.

__________. "Trinity and World Religions: Some Reflections on a Recent Book." *Clergy Monthly,* 35 (Feb., 1971) pp. 77-80.

__________. Review of *The Intra-Religious Dialogue,* by Panikkar, in *Vidyajyoti* (December 1979) p. 537.

__________. Review of *The Unknown Christ of Hinduism: Towards an Ecumenical Christophany,* by R. Panikkar, in Vidyajyoti (May-June 1982) pp. 256-257.

EARLING, B. Review of *Myth, Faith and Hermeneutics,* by Panikkar, in *Dialogue,* 21 (Winter 1982) pp. 67-68.

ÉTIENNE, J. Review of *Le Culte et l'homme Séculier,* by Panikkar, in *Revue Theologique Louvain,* 8, no., 1, p. 87.

FARRELLY, M. Review of *The Trinity and the Religious Experience of Man*, by Panikkar, in *American Ecclesiastical Reviews*, 168 (Oct., 1974) pp. 568-569.

FISKE, A. Review of *The Vedic Experience: Mantramanjari*, by Panikkar, in *Cross Currents*, 27 (Fall, 1977) p. 337.

FITTIPALDI, S. Review of *Myth, Faith and Hermeneutics*, by Panikkar, in *Horizons* (CTS) 8 (Spring 1981) 122-125.

--Also Panikkar (Rejoinder) in *Horizons*, 8 (Spring 1981) pp. 132-134

Review of *The Unknown Christ of Hinduism: Towards An Ecumenical Christophany*, by Panikkar, in *Journal of Ecumenical Studies*, 19 (Fall 1982) pp. 827-828.

FORD, J. Review of *El Silencio del Dios*, by Panikkar, in *Journal of Ecumenical Studies*, 9 (Summer 1972) p. 614.

FRISON, P. Review of *Le Christ et l'hindouisme*, by Panikkar, in *Etudes* 337 (Oct. 1972) p. 480.

HANUS, J. Review of *Blessed Simplicity: The Monk as Universal Archetype*, by Panikkar, in *Spirituality Today*, 35 (Summer 1983) p. 186.

HEALY, K. Sr. Review of *Blessed Simplicity: The Monk as Universal Archetype*, by Panikkar, in *Review for Religious*, 42 (Sept-Oct. 1983) p. 790.

HOCKEN, P. Review of *Worship and Secular Man*, by Panikkar, in *Clergy Review*, 59 (Dec. 1974) pp. 839-841.

HOLSTEIN, H. Review of *Le Mystère du Culte dans l'Hindouisme et le Christianisme*, by Panikkar, in *Etudes*, 335 (Oct. 1971) p. 476.

HOPKINS, S. Review of *The Unknown Christ of Hinduism: Towards an Ecumenical Christophany*, by Panikkar, in *Cross Currents* 31 (Summer 1981) Pp. 214-216.

HOOKER, R H. Review of *The Unknown Christ of Hinduism: Towards An Ecumenical Christophany*, by Panikkar, in *International Bulletin of Missionary Research*, 7 (April 1983) p. 80.

KAUFMAN, P L. Review of *Myth, Faith and Hermeneutics*, by Panikkar, in *Journal of Psychology and Theology*, 10 (Sum. 1982) p. 183.

KING, U. Review of *The Vedic Experience: Mantramanjari*, by Panikkar, in *Teilhard Review*, 13 (Winter 1978) p. 138.

KITAGAWA, J M. Review of *Myth, Faith and Hermeneutics*, by Panikkar, in *Anglican Theological Review*, 64 (April 1982) pp. 254-258.

KNITTER, P.F. Review of *The Intra-Religious Dialogue*, by Panikkar, in *Horizons* (CTS), 7 (Spring 1980) pp. 152-153.

KNITTER, P. Review of *Myth, Faith and Hermeneutics*, by Panikkar, in *Horizons* (CTS) 8 (Spring 1981) 126-127.

-Also Panikkar (Rejoinder) in *Horizons*, 8 (Spring 1981) pp. 132-134.

LANE, R. Review of *Blessed Simplicity: The Monk as Universal Archetype*, by Panikkar, in *Sisters Today*, 54 (January 1983) p. 309.

LANGLEY, M S. Review of *The Unknown Christ of Hinduism: Towards An Ecumenical Christophany*, by Panikkar, in *Churchman: a Quarterly Journal of Anglican Theology*, 95, no., 4 (1981) pp. 367-368.

LEEMING, B. REVIEW of *The Unknown Christ of Hinduism*, by Panikkar, in *Clergy Review*, 52 (Sep., 1967) pp. 737-739.

MASCALL, E. Review of *The Trinity and the Religious Experience of Man: Icon - Person - Mystery*, by Panikkar, in *Month*, 7 (April 1974) pp. 554-555.

MASSON, J. Review of *The Unknown Christ of Hinduism*, by Panikkar, in *Nouvelle Revue Theologique*, 98 (Dec. 1966) p. 116.

MASSON, J. Review of *Le Mystère du Culte dans l'Hindouisme et le Christianisme*, by Panikkar, in *Nouvelle Revue Theologique*, 93 (Aug-Sep., 1971) p. 731.

McDERMOTT, R. Review of *The Unknown Christ of Hinduism*, by Panikkar, in *Cross Currents*, 16 (Spring 1966) pp. 243-245.

MITRA, K. Review of *The Trinity and the Religious Experience of Man*, by Panikkar, in *Journal of Ecumenical Studies*, 12 (Spring 1975) pp. 274-275.

MITRA, K. Review of *The Intra-Religious Dialogue*, by Panikkar, in *Journal of Ecumenical Studies*, 16 (Fall 1979) p. 768.

MITRA, K., Review of *Myth, Faith and Hermeneutics*, by Panikkar, in *Horizons* (CTS), 8 (Spring 1981) pp. 127-129.

--Also Panikkar R. (Rejoinder) in *Horizons*, 8 (Spring 1981) pp. 132-134.

NOSSENT, G. Review of *Le Culte et l'homme Séculier*, by Panikkar, in *Nouvelle Revue Theologique*, 98 (Sep-Oct. 1976) p. 762.

O'CONNOR, M. Sr. Review of *The Trinity and the Religious Experience of Man*, by Panikkar, in *Sisters Today*, 46 (June-July 1975) p. 612.

PADOUX, A. Review of *The Unknown Christ of Hinduism: Towards An Ecumenical Christophany*, by Panikkar, in *Archives de Sciences Sociales de Religions*, 28 (April-June 1983) pp. 263-264.

PENNINGTON, M. Review of *The Trinity and the Religious Experience of Man*, by Panikkar, in *Review for Religious*, 33 (Summer 1974) p. 1215.

PODGORSKI, F. Review of The Intra-Religious Dialogue, by Panikkar, in *Cross Currents*, 29 (Summer 1979) pp. 231-232.

PODGORSKI, F. Review of The Intra-Religious Dialogue, by Panikkar, in *Theological Studies*, 40 (Dec., 1979) p. 798

PODGORSKI, F. Review of *Myth, Faith and Hermeneutics*, by Panikkar, in *Cross Currents* 29 (Summer 1979) pp. 231-236.

RAMISCH, J. Review of *Myth, Faith and Hermeneutics*, by Panikkar, in *Horizons* (CTS), 8 (Spring 1981) pp. 129-131.

--Also Panikkar (Rejoinder) in *Horizons*, 8 (Spring 1981) pp. 132-134.

REINHART, P. Review of *Blessed Simplicity: The Monk as Universal Archetype*, by Panikkar, in *Epiphany*, 4 (Winter 1983) pp. 110-113.

REISER, W. Review of *The Unknown Christ of Hinduism: Towards an Ecumenical Christophany*, by Panikkar, in *Heythrop*, 23 (October 1982) p. 451.

RÉTIF, A. Review of Lettre sur l'Inde, by Panikkar, in *World Justice*, 6 (Dec. 1964) p. 221.

REVIEW of *The Unknown Christ of Hinduism*, by Panikkar, in *The Irish Ecclesiastical Record*, 104 (Aug-Sep. 1965) pp. 181-182.

REVIEW of *The Unknown Christ of Hinduism: Towards an Ecumenical Christophany*, by Panikkar, in *Bibliografia Missionaria* XLVI (1982) p. 294.

REVIEW of *The Unknown Christ of Hinduism: Towards an Ecumenical Christophany*, by Panikkar, in *Social Justice*, 73 (Sept-Oct., 1982) p. 159.

REVIEW of *Lettre sur l'Inde*, by Panikkar, in *Cristian World*, 8 (1963) p. 538.

REVIEW of *Lettre sur l'Inde*, by Panikkar, in *Lumen*, 19 (Sep. 1964) p. 592.

REVIEW of *Kultmysterium in Hinduismus und Christentum: Ein Beitrag zur vergleichenden Religionstheologie.* by Panikkar, in *Bibliographia Missionaria* XXXVII (1973), p. 172.

REVIEW of *The Trinity and the Religious Experience of Man*, by Panikkar, in *Heythrop Journal*, 16 (Jan. 1975) p. 114.

REVIEW of *The Vedic Experience. Mantraman~jarí: An Anthology of the Vedas for Modern Man and Contemporary Celebration*, by Panikkar, in *The Indian Journal of Theology* 27 (1978) pp. 89-101.

RICHARDS, M. Review of *The Trinity and the Religious Experience of Man*, by Panikkar, in *Tablet*, 228 (August 31, 1974) p. 842.

ROGERS, A M S. Review of *The Unknown Christ of Hinduism: Towards An Ecumenical Christophany*, by Panikkar, in *Ching Feng: Quarterly Notes on Christianity and Chinese Religions and Culture* (English Ed.), 26, no., 1 (April 1983) pp. 63-64.

SALIBA, J. Review of *Myth, Faith and Hermeneutics*, by Panikkar, in *Horizons* (CTS), 4 (Fall 1977) p. 285.

--Also in Theological Studies, 41 (Dec. 1980) p. 810.

SAMARTHA, S J. Review of *The Unknown Christ of Hinduism: Towards An Ecumenical Christophany*, by Panikkar, in *Religion and Society*, 30 (Mar. 1983) p. 52-61.

SCHEEN, F. Review of *The Unknown Christ of Hinduism*, by Panikkar, in *World Mission*, 16 (Summer 1965) pp. 102-104.

SEASOLTZ, K. Review of *Worship and Secular Man*, by Panikkar, in *The Jurist*, 34 (Winter-Spring 1974) pp. 230-232.

SMITH, M. Review of *The Vedic Experience: Mantramanjari*, by Panikkar, in *Journal of Ecumenical Studies*, 16 (Spring 1979) pp. 344-346.

SMITH, W C. Review of *The Intra-Religious Dialogue*, by Panikkar, in *International Bulletin of Missionary Research*, 5 (April 1981) pp. 89-90.

TUGWELL, S. Review of *Le Mystère du Culte dans l'Hindouisme et le Christianisme*, by Panikkar, in *New Blackfriars*, 53 (May 1972) pp. 237-238.

TUGWELL, S. Review of *The Vedic Experience: Mantramanjari*, by Panikkar, in *New Blackfriars*, 59 (Dec. 1978) p. 573.

TURCHETTO, G. Review of *Myth, Faith and Hermeneutics*, by Panikkar, in *Cross Currents*, 30 (Fall 1980) p. 290.

TWOMEY, J. Review of *Worship and Secular Man*, by Panikkar, in *The Furrow*, 24 (Aug. 1973) pp. 518-519.

TWOMEY, J. Review of *The Trinity and the Religious Experience of Man*, by Panikkar, in *The Furrow*, 25 (Nov. 1974) p. 633-634.

VALLÉE, G. Review of *Le Mystère du Culte dans l'Hindouisme et le Christianisme*, by Panikkar, in *Theological Studies*, 34 (March 1973) p. 184.

VETTER, TILMANN. "Weltgespräch der Relilgionen. Eine Rezension." Review of *Die Verantwortung des Menschen für eine bewohnbare Welt im Christentum, Hinduismus und Buddhismus*, by Panikkar and Walter Strolz, in *Zeitschrift für Missionswissenschaft und Religions Wissenschaft* 7 (Münster 1987) pp. 137-140.

WHITE, J. Review of *Worship and Secular Man*, by Panikkar, in *Worship*, 47 (Jun-Jul. 1973) p. 376.

WICKER, B. Review of *Worship and Secular Man*, by Panikkar, in *Tablet*, 227 (April 1973) p. 339.

WILLIAMS, M. Review of *Myth, Faith and Hermeneutics*, by Panikkar, in *Clergy Review*, 66 (Summer 81) p. 337.

WOLANIN A. Review of *The Unknown Christ of Hinduism: Towards an Ecumenical Christophany*, by Panikkar, in *Gregorianum*, 65, no., 3-2 (1984) p. 539.

ZAGO, M. Review of *Le Mystère du Culte dans l'Hindouisme et le Christianisme*, by Panikkar, in *Revue de l'universite d'Ottawa*, 43 (Jan-Mar. 1973) p. 166.

C. *Other Sources: Books and Articles Consulted*

ABBA, R. "Name," in *The Interpreter's Dictionary of the Bible*, Vol., 3, edited by George Arthur Buttrick. Nashville (USA): Abingdon Press (1962) 1982, pp. 500-508.

ABÉCASSIS, ARMAND. "Le Midrach entre le Mythos et le Logos." *Les Etudes Philosophiques* (April-June 1984) pp. 189-204.

AIYANGAR NARAYAN, *Ancient Hindu Mythology*. New Delhi: Deep & Deep Publications, 1983.

ALFARO, JUAN. "II. Faith." in K. Rahner, ed. *Encyclopedia of Theology: A Concise Sacramentum Mundi*. London: Burns & Oates, (1975) 1981. pp. 500-510.

AMALADOSS, A. "Symbol and Mystery." *Journal of Dharma* 2 (October 1977): pp. 382-396.

AMALORPAVADASS. Ed., *Research Seminar on Non-Biblical Scriptures*, Bangalore: NBCLC, 1975.

ANDERSON, A.A. *New Century Bible (Based on the Revised Standard Version): Psalms Volume I*. London: Oliphants, 1972.

ANDERSON, GARY. and LUDWIG, NITA. eds. "Cult of the meta-machine: the coming computerized world." *Epiphany* [special issue] 4 (Fall 1982) pp. 1-136.

ANDERSON, GERALD H., and STRANSKY, THOMAS F., C.S.P., *Mission Trends No., 5: Faith Meets Faith*: (Lively Opinions from four Continents about Christian witness in the encounter with people of other faiths), New York:

Paulist Press, 1981.

AQUINAS, THOMAS St., *Summa Theologica* Vol., I., English ed., Westminster: Christian Classics, (1911) 1981.

__________. *Summa Theologica* Vol., II., English ed., Westminster: Christian Classics, (1911) 1981.

__________. *Summa Theologica* Vol., III., English ed., Westminster: Christian Classics, (1911) 1981.

__________. *Summa Theologica* Vol., IV., English ed., Westminster: Christian Classics, (1911) 1981.

__________. *Summa Theologica* Vol., V., English ed., Westminster: Christian Classics, (1911) 1981.

ARNASON, JOHANN P. "Progress and Pluralism: Reflections on Agnes Heller's Theory of History." *Praxis International* 3 (1984) pp. 423-437.

ATHANASIUS, St., *Letter on the Opinion of Dionysius.* Selected and translated by William A. Jurgens, *The Faith of the Early Fathers* Vol., I. Minnesota: the Liturgical Press, 1970, pp. 325-326.

__________. *Discourses Against the Ariens*, selected and translated by William A. Jurgens, *The Faith of the Early Fathers* Vol., I. Minnesota: The Liturgical Press, 1970, pp. 326-334.

__________. *Sermon to the Newly Baptized*, selected and translated by William A. Jurgens, *The Faith of the Early Fathers* Vol., I. Minnesota: The Liturgical Press, 1970, pp. 345-346.

AUGUSTINE OF HIPPO, St., *Against a Discourse of the Arians*, selected and translated by William A. Jurgens, *The Faith of the Early Fathers* Vol., III. (Minnesota: The Liturgical Press, 1970) p. 130- 131.

AYKARA, THOMAS A., Ed., *Meeting of Religions: New Orientations and Perspectives.* Bangalore: Dharmaram Publications published for Indian and Inter-Religious

Studies, Rome, 1978.

BANERJEE, K.K. "The Meaning of History." in *Logic, Ontology and Action*, edited by H. D. Lewis. Atlantic Highlands Humanities Press, 1982. pp. 1-14.

BAXTER, ANTHONY. "The Term `archetype', and its application to Jesus Christ." *The Hythrop Journal* XXV (1984) pp. 19-38.

BEANE, W. C. *Myth, Cult and Symbols in Sokta Hinduism: A Study of Indian Mother Goddess.* E.J. Brill Leiden, 1977.

BEATTIE, PAUL H. "A Perspective of Mythology." *Religious Humanism* 17 (Autumn 1983) pp. 173-181.

BERLIN, ERIC. "Response to Michael Sugrués: Consciousness in the Marxian Conception of History." *Auslegung* 10 (Spring-Summer 1983) pp. 37-38.

BOYD, ROBIN. *An Introduction to Indian Christian Theology.* Madras: The Christian Literature Society, (1969) 1979.

BRAATEN, CARL E. "The Uniqueness and Universality of Jesus Christ." in *Mission Trends No., 5 Faith Meets Faith: Lively opinions from four*

continents about Christian witness in the encounter with the people of other Faiths, Edited by Gerald H. Anderson and Thomas F. Stransky, C.S.P. New York: Paulist Press, 1981. pp.69-89.

BRACKEN, JOSEPH A. sj., *What are they saying about the Trinity?* New York: Paulist Press, 1979.

BRAYBROOKE, M. *The Undiscovered Christ.* Madras: CISRS, CLS, 1973.

BROCKWAY, R.W. "A Critique of Max Müller's Methodology of Mythology." *Journal of Dharma* 2 (October 1977): pp. 368-371.

BROWN, R. E., J. A. FITZMYER and R. E. MURPHY (edts) *The Jerome Biblical Commentary*. London: Geoffrey Chapman, (1969) 1984.

BOS, A. P. "Aristotle on Myth and Philosophy." *Philosophia Reformata* 48 (1983) pp. 1-18.

BULTMANN, RUDOLF. *Jesus Christ and Mythology*, New York: Charles Scribner's Sons, 1958.

CHETHIMATTAM, JOHN B. "Meaning and Scope of Interreligious Dialogue." *Jeevadhara* XI (1981) pp. 319-334.

__________. *Patterns of Indian Thought*, London: Geoffery Chapman; New York: Orbis Books, 1971.

CHIRAPPANATH, A.K. "Mantra and Yantra in Tantra." *Journal of Dharma* 2 (October 1977) pp. 409-426.

CULLMANN, OSCAR. *Christ and Time*. Philadelphia: Westminster Press, 1947.

CULLMANN, OSCAR. *Salvation in History*, New York: Harper & Row, 1967.

CYRIL OF JERUSALEM, St., *Catechetical Lectures*, 13, 33. Selected and translated by William A. Jurgens, *The Faith of the Early Fathers* Vol., I. Minnesota: the Liturgical Press, 1970, pp. 347-371.

DANIÉLOU, J. sj. *The Lord of History: Reflections on the Inner Meaning of History*. London: Longmans, Green and Co Ltd, 1958.

D'ARAGON, JEAN-LOUIS, sj. "The Apocalypse," in R. E. Brown, J. A. Fitzmyer and R. E. Murphy (edts) *The Jerome Biblical Commentary*. London: Geoffrey Chapman, (1969) 1984. 64:1-97.

DASGUPTA, SURENDRANATH, *A History of Indian Philosophy* Vol., I. Cambridge, 1922; reprint, Delhi: Montilal Banarsidass, 1975.

DE LA POTTERIE. "Jesus Christ, plénitude de la vérité." *Studio Missionalia* 33 (1984) pp. 305-324.

DE REINCOURT, AMAURY. *The Soul of India.* (U.K. 1961); Revised ed., New Delhi: Sterling Publishers, 1986.

DHAVAMONY. M. Ed., *Documenta Missionalia 5: Evangelization Dialogue and Development,* (Selected papers of the International Theological Conference: `International Theological Congress on Evangelization' Nagpur India October, 1971. Roma 1972.

"DIGNITATIS HUMANAE" (Declaration on Religious Freedom) in *The Documents of Vatican II.* New Delhi: St Paul Publication, 1966, pp. 554-570.

DUPRÉ LA TOUR, AUGUSIN. "Christologie et Religions non Chrétiennes," *Porche Orient Chrétien,* 36, no., 3-4 (1986) pp. 193-205.

DE SMET, R.V. s.j. "Towards an Indian Christology," *The Clergy Monthly* (Supplement to Vol., XXIX, June 1965): pp. 254-260.

DE URTARAN, Félix. "Muerte de Jesús y definitividad de la revelación cristiana." *Lumen* XXXIII (1984) pp. 193-222.

DUNNE, TAD, sj. "Trinity and History." *Theological Studies* 45 (1984) pp. 139-152.

DUPUIS, J., "The Cosmic Christ in the Early Fathers." *Indian Journal of Theology* (1966) pp. 106-120.

__________. "Christocentrism of Vatican II." *The Clergy Monthly,* 32 (1968) pp. 245-256.

__________. "Nagpur International Theological Conference." *The Clergy Monthly,* 35 (1971) pp. 458-471.

__________. "Western Christocentrism and Eastern Pneumatology." *The Clergy Monthly,* 35 (1971) pp. 190-198.

__________. "The salvific Value of Non-Christian Religions." In *Evangelization Dialogue and Development,*

Dhavamony ed., Roma, 1972, pp. 169-193.

__________. "The Cosmic Economy of the Spirit and the Sacred Scriptures of Religious Traditions." In *Research Seminar on Non-Biblical Scriptures*, Amalorpavadass, ed., Bangalore: NBCLC, 1975, pp. 117- 135.

ELIZABETH A. JOHNSON, C.S.J. "The Theological Relevance of the Historical Jesus: A Debate and a Thesis," *The Thomist*, 48 (1984), pp. 1-43.

ELMORE, W. T. *Dravidian God's in Modern Hinduism.* (1913); reprint, New Delhi: Asian Educational Services, 1984.

FALLON, P. sj. "For a True Dialogue Between Christians and Hindus," in *For A Dialogue With Hinduism.* Edt. Secretarius for Non- Christian, Roma, pp. 109-136.

FEDER, P.G. sj. *Messale quotidiano Dei Fedeli.* Roma: Edizione Romane Mame, (1961) 1966.

FITZMYER, J.A. sj. "The Letter to the Philippians," R. Brown, J. A. Fitzmyer and R. E. Murphy (edts) *The Jerome Biblical Commentary.* London: Geoffrey Chapman, 1984, 50:1-27.

FITZMYER, J.A. sj. "The Letter to the Romans," R. Brown, J. A. Fitzmyer and R. E. Murphy (edts) *The Jerome Biblical Commentary.* London: Geoffrey Chapman, 1984, 53:1-140.

FULLER, REGINALD H. "The Historical Jesus Outstanding Issues." *The Thomist* 48 (1984) pp. 368-382.

"GAUDIUM ET SPES" (Pastoral Constitution on the Church in the modern Word), in *The Documents of Vatican II.* New Delhi: St Paul Publication, 1966, pp. 172-280.

GANNE, Pierre. "Who do you Say that I am?" *Cross Currents*, XXXIII (1983) pp. 17-33.

GENEVIEVE, "The Iconography of Kāla-Bhairava." *Journal of Dharma* 2 (October 1977) pp. 427-438.

GREGORY I THE GREAT, POPE St., *Moral Teachings Drawn from Job*, selected and translated by William A. Jurgens, *The Faith of the Early Fathers* Vol., III. Minnesota the Liturgical Press, 1970) pp. 313- 318.

GRIFFITHS, BEDE. *The Cosmic Revelation*. Bangalore: Asian Trading Corporation, (1983) 1985.

__________. *The Marriage of East and West*. London: Collins Fount Paperbacks, (1982) 1983.

__________. *Return To The Centre*. London: Collins Fount Paperbacks, (1976) 1984.

GRILLMEIER, ALOYS sj. *Christ in Christian Tradition, Vol., 1: From the Apostolic Age to Chalcedon (AD 451)*. Great Britain: A.R.Mowbray & Co. Limited, (1965); revised ed., 1975.

__________. *Christ in Christian Tradition, Vol., 2: From the Council of Chalcedon (451) to Gregory the Great (590-604), Part One: Reception and Contradiction, The development of the discussion about Chalcedon from 451 to the beginning of the reign of Justinian*. London & Oxford: A.R.Mowbray & Co. Limited, 1987.

HAAG, HERBERT. "`Son of God' in the Language and Thinking of the Old Testament." *Concilium* 153 (3/1982) pp. 31-36.

HACKER, PAUL. "Religiöse Toleranz und Intoleranz im Hinduismus." in *Kleine Schriften*, pp. 376ff.

HAENCHEN, E. *The Acts of the Apostles* (Oxford, 1971).

HELFER, J. "Brahma Sútras," in *Abingdon Dictionary of Living Religions*, Gen. Ed. Keith Crim. Tennessee: Abingdon, 1981.

HEMPEL, J. "Psalms, Book of," in *The Interpreter's Dictionary of the Bible*, Vol., 3, edited by George Arthur Buttrick. Nashville (USA): Abingdon Press, (1962) 1982, pp. 942-958.

HILL, WILLIAM. J., O.P. "The History of God." *Theological Studies* 45 (1984) pp. 320-333.

HOBSBAWN, ERIC J. "Karl Marx et l'historie." *Diogéne*, no., 125 (1984) pp. 108-121.

HOOKER, ROGER. "Hindu Impressions of Christ and Christianity," in *Mission Trends No., 5 Faith Meets Faith: Lively opinions from four continents about Christian witness in the encounter with the people of other Faiths*, Edited by Gerald H. Anderson and Thomas F. Stransky, C.S.P. New York: Paulist Press, 1981. pp.258-263.

HOY, DAVID COUZENS. *The Critical Circle. Literature and History in Contemporary Hermeneutics.* Berkeley: University of California Press, 1978.

HUME, ROBERT ERNST. *The Thirteen Principal Upanishads.* (Translated from the Sanskrit), New Delhi: Oxford University Press, (1921) 1984.

HÜNERMANN, P. "Geschichte der Christologie-Geschicte Jesu Christi mit den Menschen?" *Theologische Quartals Schrift* 164 (1984) pp. 102-120.

ILLICKAMURY, CYPRIAN. *The Lordship of Jesus Christ: over the World and the Church: the Christological Witness of the Pastoral Constitution "Gaudium et Spes".* Bangalore: ATC, 1980.

IRENAEUS, St. *Adversus haereses*, selected and translated by William A. Jurgens, *The Faith of the Early Fathers* Vol., I. Minnesota: The Liturgical Press, 1970, pp. 84-104.

JACOBS, JONATHAN. "The Idea of Personal History." *International Philosophical Quarterly* XXIV (June 1984) pp. 179-189.

JENNI, E. "Messiah, Jewish" in *The Interpreter's Dictionary of the Bible*, Vol., 3, edited by George Arthur

Buttrick. Nashville (USA): Abingdon Press, (1962) 1982, pp. 360-365.

JOHN DAMASCENE, St., *The Source of Knowledge*, selected and translated by William A. Jurgens, *The Faith of the Early Fathers* Vol., III. Minnesota: the Liturgical Press, 1970, p. 331-344.

JOHNSON, ELIZABETH A., C.S.J. "Theological Relevance of the Historical Jesus: A Debate and a Thesis." *The Thomist* 48 (January 1984) pp. 1-43.

JURGENS, WILLIAM A. Selected and translated, *The Faith of the Early Fathers* Vol., I. Minnesota: the Liturgical Press, 1970.

JURGENS, WILLIAM A. Selected and translated, *The Faith of the Early Fathers* Vol., II. Minnesota: Liturgical Press, 1979.

JURGENS, WILLIAM A. (Selected and translated) *The Faith of the Early Fathers* Vol., III. Minnesota: Liturgical Press, 1979.

JUSTIN THE MARTYR, St. *First Apology* in W.A. Jurgens, Selected and translated *The Faith of the Early Fathers* Vol., I. Minnesota: Liturgical Press, 1970, pp. 50-57.

__________. *Second Apology* in W.A. Jurgens, selected and translated *The Faith of the Early Fathers* Vol., I. Minnesota: Liturgical Press, 1970, p. 57.

KADICHEENI, PAUL. "Religious Pluralism and the Uniqueness of Christ." (chronicle). *Journal of Dharma* 3 (January-March 1978) pp. 102-105.

KAṬHA UPANISHAD. Translated by R.E. Hume, *The Thirteen Principal Upanishads*. New Delhi: Oxford University Press, 1984, pp. 341-361.

KÄSEMANN, ERNST. *Commentary on Romans*. Great Britain: SCM Press, 1980.

KASPER, WALTER. *Jesus The Christ*, London: Burns & Oates; New York: Paulist Press, 1981.

__________. *The God of Jesus Christ*. New York: The Crossroad Publishing Company, 1988.

KEJR, VACLAV. "The Christ of the Future." *Communino Viatorum* No 1&2 (1984) pp. 1-5.

KHODR, GEORGES. "The Economy of the Holy Spirit." in *Mission Trends No., 5 Faith Meets Faith: Lively opinions from four continents about Christian witness in the encounter with the people of other Faiths*, edited by Gerald H. Anderson and Thomas F. Stransky, C.S.P. New York: Paulist Press, 1981. pp. 36-49.

KLANCK J.H., O.F.M. "Die Sakramente und der historische Jesus." *Wissenschaft Und Weisheit*, 47 (1984) pp. 1-11.

KOCHUMUTTOM, T. *Comparative Theology: Christian Thinking and Spirituality in Indian Perspective*. Bangalore: Dharmaram Publications, 1985.

KRASS, A.L., "Proclaiming the Inner Christ of Hinduism: An Interview with Paul Sudhakar." in *Mission Trends No., 5 Faith Meets Faith: Lively opinions from four continents about Christian witness in the encounter with the people of other Faiths*, Edited by Gerald H. Anderson and Thomas F. Stransky, C.S.P. New York: Paulist Press, 1981, pp.264-270.

KÜNG, HANS. "The World Religions in God's Plan of Salvation." in *Christian Revelation and World Religions*, ed. J. Neuner. London: Burns and Oates, 1967. pp. 67-122.

KÜNG, HANS, VAN ESS, J.; VON STIETENCRON, H.; and BECHERT, H. *Christentum und Welt-Religionen. Hinführung zum Dialog mit Islam, Hinduismus und Buddhismus*. München Zürich: Piper, 1984.

LASH, NICHOLAS. "`Son of God': Reflections on a Metaphor." *Concilium* 153 (3/1982) pp. 11-16.

LECLERCQ, J. "Le Christ - moine." *Studia Missionalia* 33 (1984) pp. 403-411.

LEO THE GREAT, POPE St., *The Tome of Leo: Letter of Pope Leo I To Flavian, Bishop of Constantinople.* June 13, 449 A.D. 28, 5. selected and translated by William A. Jurgens, *The Faith of the Early Fathers* Vol., III. Minnesota: the Liturgical Press, 1970, pp. 270-271.

LÉVI-STRAUSS, C. *La pensée sauvage.* Paris: Plon, 1962.

LOHSE, EDUARD. *Colossians and Philemon: A Commentary on the Epistle to the Colossians and to Philemon.* Translated by William R. Poehlmann and Robert J. Karris. Edited by Helmut Koester. Philadelphia: Fortress Press, 1971; Third Printing, 1982.

LOURDUSAMY, D. SIMON, "Meeting of Religions I - Indian Orientations," (Keynote address at the inauguration of the Centre for Indian and Inter-Religious Studies in Rome on 15th September, 1977) in *Meeting of Religions: New Orientations and Perspectives*, edt. Thomas, A. Aykara, (Bangalore: Dharmaram Publications published for Indian and Inter-Religious Studies, Rome, 1978) pp. 7-24.

LYONS, J.A. *The Cosmic Christ in Origen and Teilhard de Chardin: A Comparative Study.* Oxford University Press, 1982.

MAITRI UPANISHAD, Translated by R.E. Hume, *The Thirteen Principal Upanishads.* New Delhi: Oxford University Press, 1984, pp. 412-458.

MANICKAM, T.M. "Editorial." *Journal of Dharma* 2 (October 1977): pp. 365-367.

__________. "The `Myth of Origin', Aryan and Hebrew. A comparative interpretation." *Journal of Dharma* 2 (October

1977) pp. 397-409.

McDERMOTT, BRIAN. "Jesus Christ in Today's Faith and Theology." *Concilium* 153 (3/1982) pp. 3-10.

McDONALD, "The Kerygmatic Christology of Rudolf Bultmann," in *Christ the Lord: Studies in Christology. Presented to Donald Guthrie*, H.H.Rowdon, ed., Leiscester: Inter-Versity Press, 1982, pp. 311- 325.

MENACHERRY, CHERIYAN. *An Indian Philosophical Approach to the Personality of Jesus Christ*. Roma: Urbaniana University Press, 1986.

MENACHERRY, CHERIYAN. *„Die Herausforderung der Hindu-Kultur und –Religion für die christliche Initiation,"* in *Thomas Schreijack (Edt.) Menschwerden im Kulturwandel*, Luzern: Exodus, 1999, pp. 397-413.

MENACHERRY, CHERIYAN, *„Culture, Conversion, Baptism in the Indian Mission Context,"* Asvattha: an International Journal of Culture, Philosophy & Theology, No: 3, 10th December 2005, pp. 1-24. *http://www.asvattha.org/Data/Article003.pdf*

__________. "Patriarchal Approaches towards 'World Religions'." *Jeevadhara* XIV (March 1984) pp. 95-108.

MÜHLEN, HERIBERT. *Der Heilige Geist als Person*. Münster: Münsterliche Beitrag zur Theologie, 2nd ed., 1967.

MURPHY, JOHN W. "Foucault's Ground of History." *International Philosophical Quarterly* XXIV (1984) pp. 189-196.

NEUNER, J. *Christian Revelation and World Religions*. London: Burns and Oates, 1967.

NEUNER, J., sj. & J. DUPUIS sj., Ed., *The Christian Faith: in the Doctrinal Documents of the Catholic Church*. Bangalore: Theological Publication in India, 1973; third edition 1978.

NEWBIGIN, LESSLIE. "The Gospel Among Religions." in *Mission Trends No., 5 Faith Meets Faith: Lively opinions from four continents about Christian witness in the encounter with the people of other Faiths*, edited by Gerald H. Anderson and Thomas F. Stransky, C.S.P. New York: Paulist Press, 1981. pp. 3-19.

"NOSTRA AETATE" (Declaration on the Relation of the Church to Non- Christian Religions), in *The Documents of Vatican II*. New Delhi: St Paul Publication, 1966, pp. 548-553.

OLSON, ALAN., ed. *Myth, Symbol and Reality*. Notre Dame: University of Notre Dame Press, 1980.

ORIGEN, *De pincipiis*. Selected and translated by William A. Jurgens, *The Faith of the Early Fathers* Vol., I. Minnesota: The Liturgical Press, 1970, pp. 190-200.

PANNENBERG, W., ed. *Revelation as History*. 2nd ed. London: Sheed and Ward, 1979.

________. "Dogmatic Thesis on the Doctrine of Revelation," in *Revelation as History*, W. Pannenberg, ed., 2nd ed., London: Sheed and Ward, 1979, pp. 123-158.

PATRAPANKAL, JOSEPH. *Service and Salvation*, ed., Bangalore: Theological Publications in India, 1973.

PIERIS, ALOYSIUS. "Speaking of the Son of God in Non-Christian Cultures, e.g., in Asia." *Concilium* 153 (3/1982) pp. 65-70.

PIGGOTT, S. *Prehistoric India*, Harmondsworth, Middlesex, 1950.

QUASTEN, JOHANNES. *Patrology* Vo. I: *The beginnings of Patristic Literature. From the Apostles Creed to Irenaeus*, Westminster: Christian Classics, Inc., (1950) 1984.

________. *Patrology* Vo. II: *The Ante-Nicene Literatur After Irenaeus*, Westminster: Christian Classics, Inc., (1950) 1984.

RAMAN, N.S.S. "The Language of Myth in Religion." *Journal of Dharma* 2 (October 1977) pp. 372-381.

RAHNER, KARL. "The eternal significance of the humanity of Jesus for our relationship with God." in *Theological Investigations, Vol., 3: Theology of the Spiritual Life.* Translated by Karl-H. and Boniface Kruger. London: Darton Longman & Todd, (1967) 1987, pp. 35-46.

__________. "On the Theology of the Incarnation," in *Theological Investigations, Vol., 4: More Recent Writings.* Translated by Kelvin Smith. London: Darton, Longman & Todd, (1966) 1987, pp. 105-120.

__________. "Theology of the Symbol," in *Theological Investigations, Vol., 4: More Recent Writings*, Translated by Kelvin Smith. London: Darton, Longman & Todd, (1966) 1987, pp. 221-252.

__________. "Christianity and the Non-Christian Religions." in *Theological Investigation, Vol., 5: Later Writings.* Translated by Karl H. Kruger. London: Darton, Longman & Todd, (1966) 1984. pp. 115-134.

__________. "The Individual and the Church: Anonymous Christians," *Theological Investigations, Vol., 6: Concerning Vatican Council II.* Translated by Karl-H. and Boniface Kruger. London: Darton, Longman & Todd, (1969) 1984, pp. 390-398.

__________. "Intellectual honesty and Christian Faith," *Theological Investigations, Vol., 7: Further Theology of the Spiritual Life.* Translated by David Bourke. London: Darton, Longman & Todd, (1971) 1981, pp. 47-71.

__________. "I believe in Jesus Christ: Interpreting an article of faith." in *Theological Investigations, Vol., 9, Writings of 1965- 7*, Translated by Graham Harrison. London: Darton, Longman & Todd, (1972) 1981, pp. 165-168.

__________."Anonymous Christianity and the Missionary Task of the Church," in *Theological Investigations, Vol., 12: Confrontations 2*. Translated by David Bourke. London: Darton, Longman & Todd, (1974) 1987, pp. 161-168.

__________. "Remarks on the history of Jesus for catholic dogmatics" in *Theological Investigation, Vol., 13: Theology, Anthropology, Christology*. Translated by David Bourke. London: Darton, Longman & Todd, 1975. pp. 201-212.

__________. "Observations on the Problem of the `Anonymous Christian'", in *Theological Investigations, Vol., 14: Ecclesiology, Questions in the Church, the Church in the World*. Translated by David Bourke. London: Darton, Longman and Todd, (1976) 1987, pp. 280- 294.

__________. "Anonymous and Explicit Faith," in *Theological Investigations, Vol., 16: Experience of the Spirit, Source of Theology*. Translated by Kelvin Smith. London: Darton, Longman & Todd, 1979, pp. 52-59.

__________. "Jesus Christ in the Non-Christian Religions," in *Theological Investigations, Vol., 17: Jesus, Man, And The Church*. Translated by Margaret Kohl. London: Darton, Longman & Todd, 1981, pp. 39-50.

__________. "Christianity and the new Earth." *Theology Digest* 15 (Winter 1967) p. 281.

__________. Ed., *Encyclopedia of Theology: A Concise Sacramentum Mundi*. London: Burns & Oates, (1975) 1981.

__________. "Christology Today," in *Concilium: Religion in the Eighties: Jesus, Son of God?* Edts, Edward Schillebeeckx and Johannes-Baptist Metz. Edinburgh: T. & T. Clark LTD; New York: The Seabury Press, 1982, pp. 73-77.

__________. "Jesus Christ." in *Foundations of Christian Faith: An Introduction to the idea of Christianity*. Translated by William V. Dych. (German edition, Freiburg: Verlag Herder, 1976) New York: Crossroad, (1978) 1984. pp. 176-321.

RAULET, GE'RARD. "La Fin De La `Raison Dans L'Histoire'." *Dialogue* 22 (December 1983) pp. 631-646.

REESE, WILLIAM L. *Dictionary of Philosophy and Religion: Eastern and Western Thought.* New Jersey: Humanity press Inc., and Sussex: The Harvester Press Limited, 1980.

RICOEUR, PAUL. *The Reality of the Historical Past.* Milwankee Marquette Uni. Press, 1984.

[RJ.], "Christology and non-Christian religions," observations of "Christologie et Religions non Chrétiennes," *Porche Orient Chrétien,* 36, no., 3-4 (1986) pp. 193-205, by Augusin Dupré la Tour, in *Theology Digest,* 35, (Summer 1988), pp. 103-106.

ROBERTS, JOY H. "Two Kinds of Knowledge on Croce's Philosophy of History." *International Studies in Philosophy* 14 (Spring 1982) pp. 35-48.

ROTENSTREICH, NATHAN. "Universalism and Particularism in History." *Review of Metaphysics* 37 (Sept. 1983) pp. 21-36.

ROSSANO, PIETRO. "Christ's Lordship and Religious Pluralism." in *Mission Trends No., 5, Faith Meets Faith: Lively opinions from four continents about Christian witness in the encounter with the people of other Faiths,* Edited by Gerald H. Anderson and Thomas F. Stransky, C.S.P. New York: Paulist Press, 1981, pp.21-35.

SACNTON, THOMAS A. "Planet of the Year: What on earth are we doing," *Time: Planet of the Year, Endangered Earth,* (January 2, 1989) pp. 13-18.

SCHEFFCZYK, LEO. "Christology in the Context of Experience: On the Interpretation of Christ by E. Schillebeeckx." *The Thomist* 48 (1984) pp. 383-408.

SCHILLEBEECKX, Edward. *Jesus: An Experiment in Christology.* London: William Collins Sons & Co Ltd., and New York: The Seabury Press, Inc., 1979; London: Fount Paperbacks, 1983.

SCHILLEBEECKX, EDWARD AND METZ, JOHANNES-BAPTIST. "Jesus as Son of God" (Editorial). *Concilium* 153 (3/1982) pp. vii-ix.

SCHMITHALS, WALTER. *An Introduction to the theology of Rudolf Bultmann,* Translated by John Bowden, London: SCM Press Ltd, 1967.

SECRETARIATUS PRO NON CHRISTIANS, *For a Dialogue with Hinduism.* Milano, Roma: Editrice Anchora, n.d.

SEIFERT, JOSEPH. "Truth and History: Noumenal Phenomenology." *Diotima* 11 (1983) pp. 160-183.

SHARMA, ARVIND. "The Lost Veda and the Unknown Christ," in *The Indian Journal of Theology* 30, no., 1 (1981) pp. 24-28.

SOBRINO, JON. "A Crucified People's Faith in the Son of God." *Concilium* 153 (3/1982) pp. 23-28.

SPLETT, JÖRG. "Symbol." in K Rahner, ed. *Encyclopedia of Theology: A Concise Sacramentum Mundi.* London: Burns & Oates, (1975) 1981. pp. 1654-1657.

STEVENSON, W.T. *History as Myth.* New York: Seabury Press, 1969.

__________. "History as Myth: Some Implications for History and Theology." *Cross Currents* (Winter 1970) pp. 15-28.

STUART - FOX, MARTIN. "On The Theory of History and its Context of Discovery." *Philosophy of the Social Sciences* 13 (December 1983) pp. 401-424.

STUTLEY, MARGARET and JAMES, *A Dictionary of Hinduism: Its Mythology, Folklore and Development 1500 B.C.-A.D. 1500.* Bombay: Allied Publishers, 1977.

SURIN, KENNETH. "Revelation, Salvation, The Uniqueness of Christ And Other Religions." *Religious Studies* 19 (September 1983) pp. 323-344.

SWAMI CHIDBHAVANANDA, (commented) *The Bhagavad Gita.* Tamil Nadu: Sri Ramakrishna Tapovanam, 1979.

SWAMI KRISHNANANDA, *A Short History of Religious and Philosophic Thought in India.* India: The Divine Life Society, 1970.

TAYLOR, JOHN V. "The Theological Basis of Interfaith Dialogue," in *Mission Trends No., 5, Faith Meets Faith: Lively opinions from four continents about Christian witness in the encounter with the people of other Faiths,* Edited by Gerald H. Anderson and Thomas F. Stransky, C.S.P. New York: Paulist Press, 1981, pp. 93-110.

TAYSOR, STEVENSON, W. "History as Myth: Some Implications for History and Theology." *Cross Currents* XX (Winter, 1970) pp. 15-28.

TEASDALE, WAYNE. "Bede Griffiths and the Uniqueness of Christianity." *Communio* 11 (1984) pp. 177-185.

THE ORGANIZING COMMITTEE ALL INDIA SEMINAR. *All India Seminar on the Church in India Today, Bangalore, May 15-25, 1969, Orientation Papers.* New Delhi: The Organizing Committee C.B.C.I. Centre, 1969.

THILS, G. *Transcendence ou? Incarnation?,* Louvain, 1950.

VAN IERSEL, BAS. "`Son of God' in the New Testament." *Concilium* 153 (3/1982) pp. 37-48.

VAN BAVEL, TARSICIUS, "Chalcedon: Then and Now," in *Concilium: Religion in the Eighties: Jesus, Son of God?* Edts

Edward Schillebeeckx and Johannes-Baptist Metz. Edinburgh: T. & T. Clark LTD; New York: The Seabury Press, 1982, pp. 55-62.

VAWTER, BRUCE, cm., "The Gospel According to John," in *Jerom Biblical Commentary*, edts, Brown, R. E., J. A. Fitzmyer and R. E. Murphy, (London: Geoffrey Chapman, [1969] 1984), 63:1-186.

VINCENT OF LERINS, St., *Notebooks*, selected and translated by William A. Jurgens, *The Faith of the Early Fathers* Vol., III. Minnesota: the Liturgical Press, 1970, pp. 261-266.

VITSAXIS, VASSILIS G. *Hindu Epics, Myths and Legends in Popular Illustrations*. Oxford: Oxford University Press, 1977; reprint, New Delhi: Oxford University Press, 1984.

VON LEYDEN, WOLFGANG. "Categories of Historical Understanding." *History and Theory* 23 (1984) pp. 53-77.

WALKER, IAN. "Professor Wiles on Historical Christology." *New Blackfriars* 60 (1979) pp. 52-61.

WAINWRIGHT, GEOFFREY. "`Son of God' in Liturgical Doxologies." *Concilium* 153 (3/1982) pp. 49-54.

WIEDERKEHR, DIETRICH. "`Son of God' and `Sons of God': The Social Relevance of the Christological Title." *Concilium* 153 (3/1982) pp. 17-22.

WILSON, TOM. Christian Responses to Five Views of the Bhagavad Gita: Entry into Dialogue, Newcastle upon Tyne: Cambridge Scholars Publishing, 2021

WOLFSON, H.A. *The Philosophy of the Church Fathers.* Vol., I., Cambridge, Mass: Harvard University Press, 2nd. ed., 19